THE MAN OF FASHION

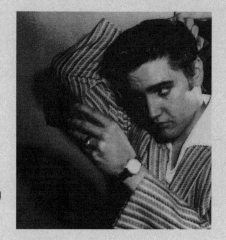

COLIN McDOWELL

THE MAN
OF FASHION

PEACOCK MALES AND PERFECT GENTLEMEN

with more than 250 illustrations, 99 in colour

THAMES AND HUDSON

TO JEREMY COOKE

Picture Research: GEORGINA BRUCKNER

PAGE ONE: A French dandy. Engraving, Paris, 1845
PAGE TWO: *Left to right:* French courtier, engraving by Abraham Bosse, Paris, 1633;
Caricature of Bulwer Lytton by Daniel Maclise, London, 1832; Elvis Presley combing his hair

Text © 1997 Colin McDowell
Layout © 1997 Thames and Hudson Ltd, London

British Library Cataloguing-in-Publication Data
A catalogue record for this book is available from the British Library

ISBN 0-500-01797-2

Printed and bound in Singapore by C.S. Graphics

CONTENTS

OPPOSITE: Domenico Veneziano, *The Adoration of the Magi* (detail), *c.* 1400–1461

MASCULINE CURVES

A man's bottom is the only part of his anatomy to rival the female shape for curvaceousness. It has always been considered an erogenous zone, normally kept decently covered but occasionally allowed to burst out into glorious sexuality. Whenever it does, the moralists become nervous. In fifteenth-century Europe, tight hose and short jackets were considered such a danger to morality that Church and State tried hard to kill the fashion. The combination resurfaced in the late twentieth century with skintight jeans and blouson jackets, which in the drawings of Tom of Finland become unequivocally homoerotic. But tight jeans appeal to heterosexual men as much as they do to gays and are worn with the confidence with which young men in Western Samoa display the scarification of their skin, which is worked on and improved over many years. No matter how the design of trousers might fluctuate, tight jeans are a fashion which is unlikely to be forsaken.

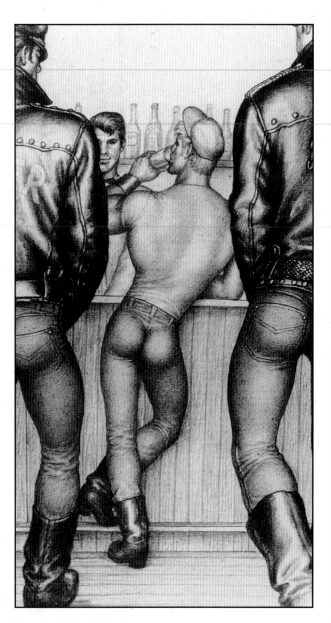

Illustration by Tom of Finland, 1965

Detail from *The Story of Griselda*, anonymous, *c.* 1500

OPPOSITE: Tattooed man, Western Samoa, 1990

SLASH

The origin of the slashing craze is lost in history. Theories abound, the most popular being that it originated with the military – the source of so much male fashion. The *Landsknechte* were medieval mercenaries who travelled across Europe, selling their skills to kings, princes and emperors. They lived outside the normal bounds of society and made their own rules. Their practice of slashing their garments to render themselves more intimidating was taken up by tailors, who saw the layered effect it produced as the perfect answer to their customers' requests for increasing extravagance and opulence in their dress. Slashing became a strong fashion statement across Europe in the early sixteenth century but it was not until the 1980s that it re-emerged with the Punks, who also saw themselves as unbounded by convention.

The Death of St Peter Martyr, Brescian School, 16th century

OPPOSITE TOP LEFT AND BACKGROUND PICTURE: Sachez Coello (1642–93), *Don John of Austria*

LEFT, TOP: Lucas Cranach, *Henry the Pious, Duke of Saxony*, 1514

LEFT, BOTTOM: Punk, early 1980s

UNDERWEAR

It is only since the 1950s that underwear for men has ceased to be entirely utilitarian and has become an erotic item of dress. Before that time underwear was worn solely for hygienic purposes. The change from sanitary to sexual motivation began in the United States in the 1920s when the firm Cooper's, of Kenosha, Wisconsin, created the Y-front for sportsmen.

The sight of a man in his underwear – traditionally ludicrous – has been a staple of farce for generations. Baggy and all-concealing, such clothing robbed the male of dignity by making him comical. Underwear came to be seen as expressing male sexual power only when it became body-conscious – a move begun by Cooper's, carried on with fifties briefs and posing pouches and brought to a climax by Calvin Klein in the eighties.

Yves Saint Laurent's underpants have an eroticism of buttons and are cut to follow the contours of buttocks and thighs – further accentuated by seams. The sensuality of such underwear is not meant to be enjoyed by the wearer alone.

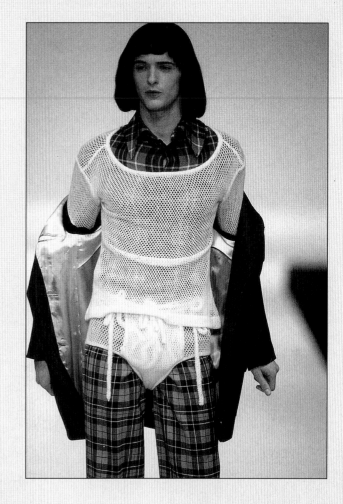

TOP: Advertisement for Rasurel underwear, 1950s, France

RIGHT: Vivienne Westwood, 1997–98

OPPOSITE: Advertisement for Yves Saint Laurent underwear, 1996

14

CODPIECES

Masculine power has always been linked to virility. This has been made manifest in many ways, but never more showily than in Renaissance fashionable dress. Broad shoulders, well-turned legs and trim waists all suggested the athletic man of action. But the most powerful symbol of male power was the codpiece, surely the most bizarre of all developments in male dress. Originally practical and protective, its padding eventually reached such proportions that it became the focal point of a man's appearance. Although aggressive and eye-catching, its main purpose was not sexual. The codpiece was a warning shot to men, not an invitation to women. Its message was unequivocal: I am the man in charge here and if you want to change that situation, be prepared to fight.

BELOW: Luca Signorelli, Detail of soldiers from the fresco *The Last Judgment*, Orvieto Cathedral, 1499-1504

OPPOSITE: Jacob Seisenegger, *The Emperor Charles V,* mid-16th century

RIGHT: Vivienne Westwood, 1996

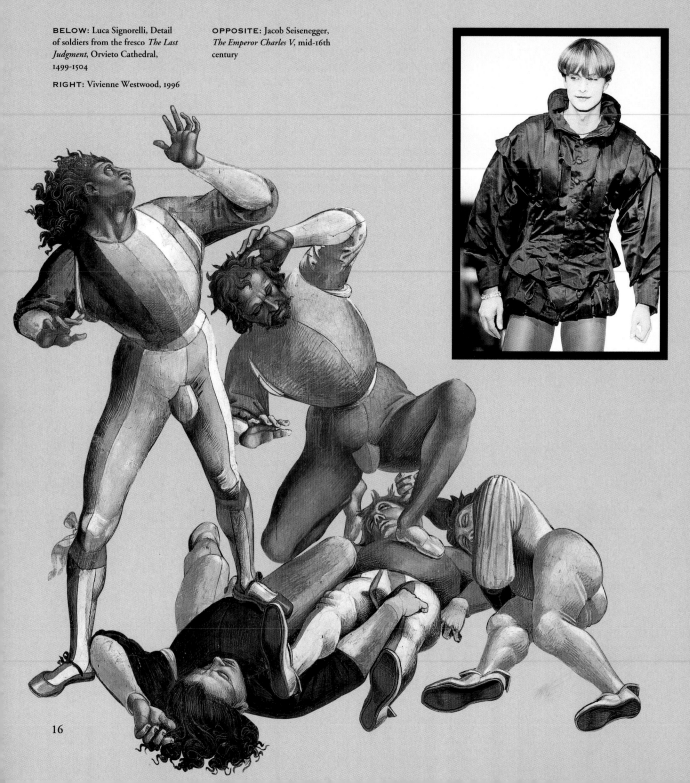

LACE

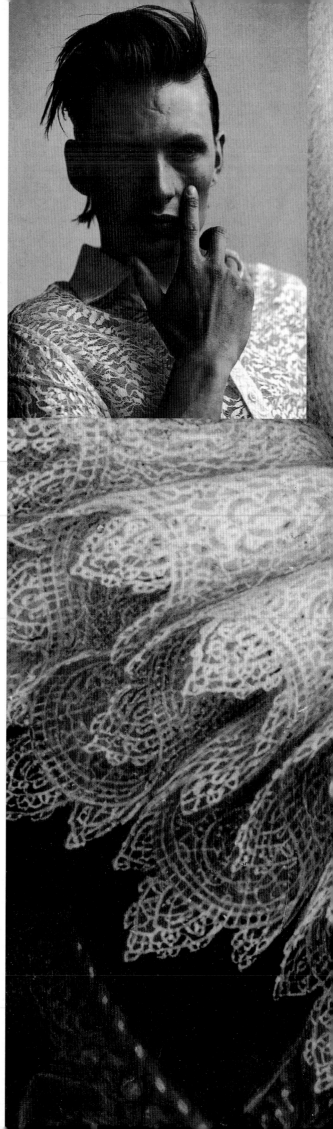

The semiotics of lace have varied over the centuries. In the sixteenth century, it represented the status and wealth of the fashionable courtier. By the seventeenth it was the mark not only of the man of mode but also of the man worthy of respect, be he government official, successful merchant or hereditary peer. The middle and upper classes took lace for granted, though its quality was keenly noted. Equally as important was the quantity of starch used to keep it crisp. The sixteenth-century chronicler Philip Stubbes writes of 'great and monstrous ruffs...some a quarter of a yard deep'. In ecclesiastical dress lace stood for purity and delicacy. Today, the lace story for men is much more complex, involving purity and perversity in a cross-dressing cocktail of sexual subversiveness which appeals to men confident of their sexuality, whatever its orientation.

ABOVE: Francesco Trevisani, *Cardinal Ottoboni, c.* 1700–1702

TOP RIGHT: Richard Tyler, 1996

RIGHT: Isaac Oliver, *Henry, Prince of Wales,* 1612

THIS PAGE: Three
details from *Louis XIV*,
French School, *c.* 1675

THE SUN KING

When a king is robed his dress must reflect his exalted position, whether it is part of an elaborate allegory of kingship or merely emphasizes the trappings of worldly invulnerability. The richest brocades, finest furs, most vibrant velvets – all embroidered and bejewelled – are used to cow the onlooker by their sheer magnificence.

No king ever again presented himself with the glamour and glitter with which Louis XIV dressed at Versailles, a court in which the minutiae of dress codes became an almost daily study as courtiers avidly searched for clues as to what was to be the next fashion.

If the male fashion victim is to be found anywhere, it is at Versailles, where courtiers were led in a complicated stylistic dance by a king whose attitudes might appear capricious but were in fact rigidly bound by a protocol whose purpose was to exalt his own appearance over that of all others.

In their attempt to please, courtiers beggared themselves, neglected and bled dry their estates, and eventually pulled France down to such a level that Revolution seemed the only way out. Vanity has never had to pay so high a price.

BELOW AND BACKGROUND:
Details from Jean Nocret,
The Family of Louis XIV,
c. 1670

HIGH STYLE

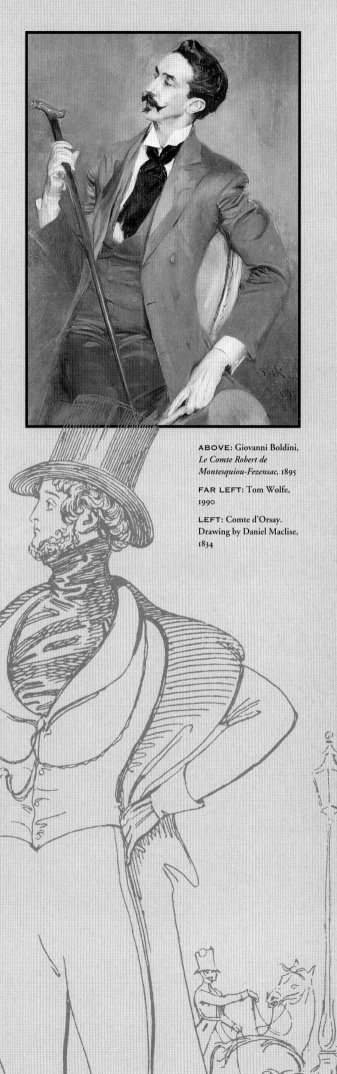

The components of masculine high style are remarkably consistent. Since the early nineteenth century, they have varied little. Fine linen, the most immaculate cuffs prominently to the fore, waistcoats, exuberant ties and cravats are as important as impeccably cut coats and trousers. The outline is slim and streamlined – the dandy is the Concorde of the male dress world. Even if certain ingredients such as cravats, walking sticks and gloves have lost prominence, there is not a dandy here who would not immediately recognize his kind even when separated by more than 150 years. And the answering call to which they respond over the years is not merely sartorial. It is equally to do with bearing, a form of self-presentation which creates a *cordon sanitaire* between the body exquisite and the *hoi polloi*.

This distance, and the fastidiousness of the perfectionist, are what give the dandy an air of frigidity, heightened by his natural tendency to strike a pose. With the exception of Tom Wolfe, all the men here are self-consciously 'on show', and even he looks more than a little self-aware, standing before a poster surely chosen to emphasize his own sartorial statement.

ABOVE: Giovanni Boldini, *Le Comte Robert de Montesquiou-Fezensac*, 1895

FAR LEFT: Tom Wolfe, 1990

LEFT: Comte d'Orsay. Drawing by Daniel Maclise, 1834

OPPOSITE, MAIN PICTURE: Benjamin Disraeli. Drawing by Daniel Maclise, 1833

OPPOSITE TOP LEFT: Gabriel D'Annunzio, *c.* 1900

OPPOSITE BOTTOM LEFT: Boniface, Comte de Castellane-Novejean (Boni de Castellane), 1923. Photo by Paul Nadar

OPPOSITE TOP RIGHT: Patrick Lichfield, 1969

· SVÆ · XLIX ·

COURTLY GLORIES

Sir Walter Scott has a lot to answer for. If today we think of the Middle Ages and the Age of Chivalry as a time when knights were not only bold but also pure of heart, refined in their manners and clean in their persons, it is largely his fault.

In fact, most medieval knights must have been simple, coarse men, for much of the time as rough in dress as in speech. And as for cleanliness, even at the beginning of the thirteenth century, Philip Augustus, King of France, changed his apparel only three times a year, as did the princes of his household.

But things advanced quickly. By the end of the century, the French court was famous – even notorious – for its luxuries. Soon the influence of French styles of dress and behaviour was being felt in every court in Christendom. France had become the crucible of the fashionable world, with men of style from all of Europe's courts and prosperous cities demanding the latest and most international fashions, as sanctioned by Paris.

To service their needs, the trade in textiles took second place only to that in foodstuffs. Vast quantities of cotton, linen, wool and silk were moved across the known world in their raw state before cleansing and weaving converted them into the materials of vanity and they moved on again to be crafted into the kind of clothing that was essential to the increasingly important matter of creating the correct impression. And, regardless of which country his court might be in, the man of power knew his sources. Wool from England and linen from Rheims were the best; silks had to be Italian, preferably from Lucca or Florence, though those of Genoa were also acceptable; and the only dyes to meet with full approval were from Asia.

OPPOSITE: Hans Holbein (1497–1543), *Portrait of Henry VIII*

Such were the raw materials to be worked on by tailors, hatters, glovers, shoemakers, embroiderers and weavers whose numbers and skills increased annually to fulfil the demands of an insatiable courtly class whose influence stretched across Europe and affected clergy and merchant, young and old, in a society in which every man viewed his fellow as a rival. Add to these the furs of Scandinavia and Russia, the precious pelts of Asia and the Arctic, the quality leathers of England, Spain and Portugal, the feathers and 'dalliance' of Italy and France, and the picture of the perfected man of pleasure emerges.

But he does not command the stage unchallenged. Jostling for the limelight – and equally as impressive in appearance – is the man of wealth and political pretension, first in a line of peacock males for whom gorgeous garb is not a trivial pastime but a magnificent setting for the jewel of power and ambition. In all cases, wealth and power went hand in hand with display, and nowhere was this more clearly visible than in the outward show of the Church, which not only played the worldly game, but sanctioned it in others by its own luxury and magnificence. Holy Rome itself was notorious for its lust not only for gold but for the best of everything the world had to offer. Matthew Paris, writing his *Chronica Majora* in 1246, notes that Pope Innocent IV,

> having noticed that the ecclesiastical ornaments of certain English priests…were embroidered in gold thread after a most desirable fashion…sent letters, blessed and sealed, to wellnigh all the abbots of the Cistercian order established in England, desiring that they should send him without delay those embroideries of gold which he preferred above all others.

What could secular men do but follow the Church's lead? And what was left to kings but to vie with one another for magnificence? A contemporary inventory listed Charles V of France's best robes as including seven six-piece suits furred with ermine; seven three-piece suits furred with miniver and sixteen parts of suits also furred with miniver. Miniver – the underbelly of the common grey squirrel – was, despite its humble origins, regularly subject to sumptuary laws. These regulations, through which monarchs

The Coronation of the Emperor Frederick III by Pope Nicholas V in 1452,
anonymous Flemish painting

tried to keep the trappings of power to themselves, precluded the wearing of certain materials, colours and skins by all not royal born or of courtly status. The statute books of Europe were littered with such laws, as ineffectual as they were pompous. The English kings were especially fond of them: in one session of parliament alone, Edward III passed eight sumptuary laws. It was a pattern which would continue, with more or less severity, well into the sixteenth century.

Were these laws really necessary? Were so many men in love with gaudy show? There are enough contemporary descriptions to suggest that plenty were. The medieval writer Fabian describes in his *Chronicles* how the rot spread even to the clergy, whom he criticized for their 'bushed and braided heads, long-tailed gowns, blazing clothes, shining golden girdles...gilt spurs...and divers other enormities'.

As in any society which extols virility to a point where it becomes a fetish, medieval Europe was haunted and excited by the spectre of sodomy. Virile young men, in love with their masculinity and banded together in inward-looking groups which excluded most other men and all women, dressed, if not to attract members of their group sexually, then certainly to obtain their admiration and approbation. The dangers inherent in hero worship within a closed society where all members were, in fact, heroes and, in a sense, self-worshipping, were not lost on outsiders – not only the chroniclers but also the old and worthy whose role it was to regulate

societies which often had only the most precarious of footholds on civil order and control. The Church had long ago convinced them that untrammelled sexuality led to sedition, outrage and the collapse of society. In homosexuality – whether overt or hidden – the dangers were deemed greater.

It is for this reason that the love of finery was inevitably condemned as effeminate, and extravagance in dress usually treated as an aberration. In the reign of Henry II, the scholar John of Salisbury even castigated the Knights Templar (who with their vows of piety and poverty had been seen as the perfection of chivalrous masculinity) for their addiction to finery and personal decoration. He accused them of seeing war merely as an excuse for display, their costumes 'exciting the ire of the sober minded'. 'A feminine taste reigned', he wrote, so that 'many begin to doubt the sex of the wearer.' It is easy to understand why, in the light of such comments, which were by no means confined to England, there was a feeling of unease. Even as late as the fifteenth century, attempts were made in Florence to prevent young men from wearing brief jerkins and long, waved hair, for fear their appearance would encourage sodomy.

Fashionably skimpy dress exercised moralists across Europe. The *Mainz Chronicle*, referring to the year 1367, wrote, 'In those days the folly of men went so far that the younger men wore coats

ABOVE: *A Pair of Lovers*, anonymous 15th-century engraving

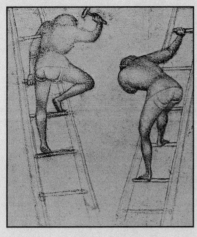

too short to provide decent covering.' It was the same in France. The *Saint-Denis Chronicle* blamed the French defeat at Crécy on divine wrath at the indecency of French dress: 'Some of them wore their coats so short that when they were forced to stoop to serve a gentleman anyone standing behind them could see their hose, as well as the anatomy beneath.' In Chaucer's 'The Parson's Tale', the cleric rails against 'the horrible disordinate scantiness of clothing…that do not cover the shameful members of man…some of them show the very boss of their shape and the horrible, swollen members.'

As is usual with moralists, a distinction was made between the status-laden dress of the wealthy man and the coxcomb fashions followed by the young. Dignity was dressed with considerable style and glamour; impudence was seen as being at the whim of any and all unsuitable sartorial crazes. There was clearly a double standard at work, a reflection of the age-old desire for the gravitas of age to be acknowledged and the fear of its being undermined by unruly, rebellious youth.

There was intense rivalry between and within the courts of Europe and magnificent dress was undoubtedly one of the major weapons in the fight for supremacy. Certainly, manufacture was sufficiently sophisticated to create gorgeous and delicate fabrics by this time. Scarlet, the name of a fine woollen material as well as a colour, was highly prized, with the best quality coming from Ghent. Velvet, either of cotton, produced in Lucca, or wool, from Venice; brocades, usually heavily embroidered in gold and silver; and, above all, silk, were considered rare and valuable stuffs and each was subject to various sumptuary injunctions at different times. These textiles were usually printed but were sometimes magnificently embroidered, mainly by nuns.

Until well into the twelfth century, the cutting and sewing of garments was undertaken by ladies of the court, who also wove the flax and wool in common daily use for dress. The nineteenth-century German historian Max von Boehm records that when King Gunther 'resolved to woo Brunhild and equipped himself for the journey, his sister Kriemhild gathered together thirty maidens with whom she toiled for six weeks in order to provide her brother…with apparel.' But, even at the beginning of the twelfth century, guilds of tailors, offering more professional services, were springing up in courts across Europe. The art of cutting – the basis of all tailoring – was developed in order to produce clothes of better fit. In response to the need for shorter, tighter jackets, shaped to the body, the number of tailors in Paris between 1292 and 1300 increased from 482 to 702, the demand for their services coming entirely from men.

Extravagance is catching. Privileged classes not only dress well in order to parade their special position, they also dress those around them with a luxury which will equally display their wealth

ABOVE: Bartolino de'Grossi (1435-64), *Two Men on a Ladder*

and power. The pride of serving men – who, in the entourage of a prince, would be high born and possibly even titled – was encouraged because, for all the railing against scarlet robes, floor-length sleeves and fur-trimmed garments, well-dressed retainers were a reflection of their master's power and generosity.

The splendour started at the top. For every dowdy king, such as Edward I (surely the most sartorially dreary of all monarchs, with his insistence upon wearing the plain garments of a citizen except on feast days, and his refusal to wear his crown after his coronation), there were peacocks a-plenty. Edward II, for example, was, according to Robert of Reading, 'fair of body and great of strength'. But he had a fatal flaw: his love of Piers Gaveston, 1st Earl of Cornwall, whom he treated initially as a brother. Captivated by Gaveston's charm, Edward allowed him liberties which infuriated his barons and eventually led to his downfall. Luxury and decadence, obsessive interest in appearance, voluptuous nights of dressing up, gifts of costly garments and jewelry all led Edward down the primrose path to ruin. The nobles viewed such behaviour with distaste. The love of finery and the playing out of fantasies became so closely allied to perversity and depravity that the upper classes would never again be able to see fashion with innocent eyes. Further, such behaviour was too feminine, too near the legitimized interest of the second sex to

be acceptable in men expected to show their credentials for ruling the world by the way they disported themselves both in private and in public. Gaveston's greed and arrogance had not only infatuated the king, they had rocked a nation. And taking too great an interest in fashion was given a bad name which it kept for centuries. The vying for ever more fantastic and extravagant styles which was the norm in Edward II's court can even be said to have started the great divide between male and female attitudes to fashionable dress. The fashion-equals-perversity equation, which has inhibited men for centuries, took hold. Male narcissism became suspect and condemned; in future, only the female sex would be allowed to love its appearance for its own sake.

The reign of Edward II was a time of undoing. The chivalrous attitudes of barons and knights, so long taken for granted, had degenerated. The nobility were no longer seen as protectors, but as plunderers. The age of feudalism was over and the day of the middle-class merchant and tradesman had arrived.

The fashion lead, once the undisputed province of Aquitaine, now moved from court to court – one being famous for one style, one for another. Indisputably above the rest, however, was the court of the cultured, creative and ruthlessly competitive Dukes of Burgundy, a centre of such brilliance that it served as the model for all others. It was famous for ceremonial etiquette and formality. The Grand Duke Philippe III – the man who offered Henry V the

crown of France – was the fashion leader of Europe, fabled for his sumptuous dress, his stupendous table and the richness of his tapestry-hung court. On state occasions and for special ceremonial visits, which could last for many days or even weeks, he was never seen in the same costume twice and changed his jewelry daily – as befitted the man known to be the wealthiest duke in Europe.

He celebrated his third marriage, to the Infanta Isabella of Portugal, by founding in 1429 the Order of the Golden Fleece – Le Toison d'Or. This immediately became the template for all Orders of Chivalry. Restricted to the sovereign and twenty knights, the order was an excellent excuse for indulging one of the Duke's passions – dressing up in the panoply of power. As Grand Master, he designed for himself a mantle of black velvet and a long surcote of crimson velvet lined with white silk and held at the waist by a heavy gold chain. It is little wonder that the Duke and his court were the envy of Europe for sophistication and assurance.

In fact the Duke created European style for years to come. It is thanks to him that exaggeration entered male fashion – exaggeration of shape, in particular. Burgundian shoulders were padded to ensure that they were wider than those of any other European court; Burgundian waists were more sharply defined, Burgundian chests more fully bombasted. In fact, Burgundian man was the cynosure of male eyes everywhere and reports of developments in his dress were eagerly circulated to pages and cup-bearers as well as to kings and princes.

Others, however, were less impressed. Beneath the outward show, moralists detected immodesty. Enguerrand de Monstrelet, chronicler of fourteenth- and early fifteenth-century Europe, complained that tight leg-coverings and the newly merged breeches and hose threw the male member into too much prominence. The braguette, or codpiece, which was to become such a feature of noble dress under the Tudors and Valois, earned his total condemnation. Nevertheless, its appeal to men

ABOVE: Miniature from Jacques de Guise's *Chroniques de Hainault,* showing Philip the Good, Duke of Burgundy, receiving the manuscript from Simon Nockart, Flemish, 1448

wishing to project an image of power was so great that it became hugely popular across Europe.

Another male fashion with distinct sexual connotations was the narrowly pointed shoe known as the poulaine, or crakowe. The style was actually recorded as early as the end of the eleventh century, when it was an immediate success with the young, who quickly began to exploit its sexual possibilities. Like any item vital to survival, footwear had long assumed an almost talismanic importance, so it is not surprising that in the late Middle Ages it produced one of the first universal, run-away fashion fads for men. And, as the toes of poulaines gradually lengthened, the style became even more desirable, providing an early demonstration of the basic fashion fact that once a fad has been created questions of comfort and convenience are not even asked. In fact, the less practical the fashion, the greater its attraction. What made the poulaine irresistible was the fact that it was so impractical that it demonstrated to all that its wearer, unlike peasants and the underprivileged, was not a worker. Such exclusiveness and snobbery are the basis of all high-fashion trends.

There was a 'bad-boy', 'bit-of-a-lad' quality to the poulaine which endeared it not only to the young, but also to more sober minds. Medieval men past the first excitements of youth also welcomed this suggestive style. Inevitably, as the fashion flourished and became universal, it grew even more extreme. The point of the toe, often stuffed and ornamented, became so inordinately long that the shoes were almost impossible to walk in, especially in the mud and slime of medieval streets. Equally inevitably, class distinction entered the fashion. Soon the degree of inconvenience and impracticality imposed by the length indicated the rank (and self-importance) of the wearer. At one period in the German courts, barons were allowed points up to two feet long whereas even the richest merchant was, in theory, limited to half that length. Either way, at this moment we find the perfect example of the impracticality of high fashion: footwear in which it is impossible to walk. The fad had gone as far as it could go and, though the long points were doubled back and secured just below the knee for greater ease of movement (a style attributed to James I of Scotland), the reign of the poulaine was over.

At times even the most careful and moderate of men find extrovert fashion hard to resist. So it was with the other late medieval fad: the craze for slashed and torn garments. For the bold fashion follower, monotone material had proved a bore and two-tone, uni-party tights had been a strong fashion among the young, especially in Italy. Red and white were the most popular colours and, as such, attracted most criticism, but any combination at all met with disapproval. The objection was to the fact that the join where the two colours met drew unnecessary attention to the male bottom and bulge. Add to this the constant outcry against the brevity of doublets and you have a classic situation in which an outsider fashion can thrive, for nothing gives a greater boost to young, iconoclastic style than social disapproval married to sexual frisson.

Once a style is universal, however, there is already a new one, known only to the cognoscenti. After uni-party, a different variation had to be found and it came from the most unexpected of sources: the soldiery.

At the beginning of the fifteenth century, the need for armed soldiers was still great. Much of a country's wealth went on a new breed of fighting men: the paid mercenaries. Cunning, unreliable and infinitely corruptible, the mercenaries' greatest joy was the sacking of rich cities. They often fought without pay on the understanding that the booty would be theirs – and the quicker the city fell to its knees, the greater their share.

Feared by all decent citizens, the mercenaries of the late fifteenth and early sixteenth century, known as *Landsknechte*, bayoneted their way across Europe. And, according to costume historians, they created a fashion sensation second only to that of the poulaine: the craze for slashed and torn clothing which would become the costume of the fashionable man in every court in Europe.

It is said that the slashing craze began with Swiss mercenaries who, having defeated Charles the Bold of Burgundy in 1477, rampaged through his camp, tearing down his magnificent silk tents in order to use the material to patch their ragged garments for their triumphant return home. So, a new fashion was born, a fashion which was taken up by German mercenaries and which then swept through France and on to England. But it is worth asking whether the motley and bedraggled appearance of mercenaries – men loathed by all sides – was likely to be adopted by refined and fastidious courtiers and whether a more credible explanation of the slashing phenomenon is not to be found in the commercial and social scenes. Rich men were contriving to use their dress to advertise their position, and what better way to do this than to pile magnificence on magnificence? What more negligent fashion gesture than to slit open a costly fabric to reveal an even costlier one beneath? And what could be more appealing to the armies of vying tailors which had sprung up in every city in Europe than to show their superior skills in the most complicated and eye-catching way possible?

The *Landsknechte* were surely not refined enough to impose a style on the wealthy without the intermediary taste of the tailors, for both court life and upper-class life had by this time become highly sophisticated. And with sophistication a new preoccupation had arrived – an obsession with cleanliness. The modern age, in which the right to a clean body and clothing has moved from a privilege, to a necessity, to a fetish, had begun. The snowy white shirt of the sixteenth century was about to be born, bringing with it the first bat-squeak of fastidiousness which, three centuries later, would entirely rout ostentation as the universal bedrock of memorable male dress.

DRESSED FOR POWER

The warring princes, disputatious dukes and vying nobles who characterized the fifteenth century would soon become less of a feature, leaving sixteenth-century Europe the firm province of kings. And what memorable kings they were to be. Henry VIII of England, Francis I of France and Charles V of Spain and the Netherlands were the very acme of the nobility and power of legitimate succession.

Of the three, Henry was the most impressive, the fashion leader who set the standard for all others. Admired across Europe for his extraordinary physique, his athleticism and his cultural accomplishments, he was spoken of in superlatives even by the ambassadors of countries to whom England was no great friend. So magnificent were his garments that they turned ambassadors, plenipotentiaries and visiting politicians into fashion writers, eager to put all the gorgeousness on paper in long and detailed descriptions to be sent back to their masters.

Most tirelessly sycophantic was the Venetian ambassador. In 1519, describing Henry playing tennis, he wrote, 'It is the prettiest thing in the world to see him play, his fair skin glowing through a shirt of the finest texture.' It is hard to believe when one reads his reports that this particular ambassador had a reputation as the most astute, shrewd and austere in judgment of all sixteenth-century diplomats. As a young man – 'Tall of stature, very well formed, and of very handsome presence' – Henry was the perfect male model of his day, the vain, brilliant

perhaps most flatteringly, 'in cloth of gold with a raised pile... like St George in person'.

Kingship is covetous. When Charles V patronized Titian, Francis I felt obliged to employ Leonardo, while Henry VIII made Holbein his court artist. So it was with dress. They all watched each other like hawks, demanding from travellers, spies and diplomats minute descriptions of the modes and manners of the others' courts.

It is instructive to read the Venetians on the rivalry between Charles and Henry when they met in London in 1520. Charles, Emperor of Germany, King of Spain, Count of Flanders and Lord of all Italy, who kept the richest court in the world, appeared in a long robe, 'the right half of cloth of silver, the left half of alternative stripes of gold and silver, all lined with costly sables'. Not to be outdone, Henry appeared in 'a robe entirely of cloth of gold, lined with very beautiful lynx fur'. Charles: 'a doublet of silver brocade and a gold robe, sable lined'. Henry: 'a doublet, one half of cloth of gold, the other of grey velvet'. Each ceremonial highpoint produced a new fashion statement. Except, of course, that these garments were nothing whatsoever to do with fashion but were the essential dress of kingdoms and empires. Two yards of cloth of gold – silk or wool in which threads of gold were woven – were seen by the world as representing immense wealth, authority and power. A shorthand for everything that makes for the singularity of kingship, they spoke more tellingly than long

sensualist rather than the bloodstained syphilitic monster he was to become. And, like all men of fashion, he was aware of international trends and keen to wear the latest style, regardless of its country of origin. The ambassador records him dressed in 'stiff brocade in the Hungarian fashion', and in 'white damask in the Turkish fashion...all embroidered with roses made of rubies and diamonds, in accordance with his emblem, a most costly costume'; also, and

lists of ordinances, funds and taxes about the superior status of a true, anointed king.

Showy as it was, the visit of Charles V to England was nothing compared with the world's first great summit conference: the meeting between Henry VIII and Francis I of France, known as the Field of Cloth of Gold and conceived as a parade of fashion which would act as a paradigm of power, a thirteen-day extravaganza of everything money could buy.

Splendour triumphed as the flower of two nations flaunted their wealth and possessions. The once barren plains of the Val d'Or shimmered with velvet, sarcenet, satin and cloth of gold. The temporary palaces erected by each side were, according to eyewitness description, hung with rich silk which made a perfect setting for the clothes, 'like bullions of fine burned gold', as Hall chronicles. He described Henry as 'in beauty and personage the most goodliest prince that ever reigned over the realm of England; his grace was apparelled in a garment of cloth of silver, of damask, ribbed with cloth of gold, so thick as might be…it was marvellous to behold.' His description of Francis, less extravagantly phrased, refers to the king's amazing cloak set with pearls and precious stones which was flung over a costume rich with cloth of silver and gold.

In true Renaissance style the two monarchs piled riches on riches. Slashed, puffed and padded, they created the fashionable shape for men, a shape that would last for more than fifty years. Its effect was to turn the body into a stiff and graceless canvas providing the maximum area for a display of uninhibited vulgarity and ostentation. Stuffed and padded manikins stalked through the courts in a bizarre game of fashion follow-my-leader, their shoulders extended, their peascod bellies protruding, their torsos elongated and, most notoriously, their codpieces rampant. The effect was heavy, ponderous and, to modern eyes, somewhat absurd, despite all the glittering outward show.

The codpiece was the crudest of all signals of raw masculine power. Called the *bragetto* in Italy, where it first appeared, it started off as a practical and utilitarian flap which covered the opening of the hose. It then began to be lightly padded as a form of protection for a vulnerable area – one not easily safeguarded, even by armour. Eventually the padding increased in size and weight to such an extent that it came more and more to resemble the male member it was meant to cloak.

There was something essentially brutal and brutalizing about the codpiece, which tells us much about the psychology of the sixteenth-century male. From the outset, its message was to men rather than women; it was concerned with social, temporal and territorial power rather than with sexual prowess.

And it fed the moralists' bile. The English writer Philip Stubbes accused his fellow countrymen of being 'poisoned by the arsenic of pride'. But such criticism – the rumblings of a new puritanism which would come to fruition in the following fifty years – could for the time being be ignored by men dedicated to self-adornment. With their clothes chests stuffed with satin, velvets, furs, feathers and lace all in the latest style; and their jewel boxes crammed with gold chains, rings, brooches, pearls and semi-precious stones, they still had time to preen, to ogle each other and, above all, to take the leisurely approach to dressing which the increasingly elaborate fashions demanded.

By the mid-sixteenth century, however, a new restraint was beginning to enter male dress. As early as 1528, Baldassare Castiglioni, the Italian diplomat, had suggested in *The Courtier*, his extremely influential treatise on courtly behaviour, that the 'raiment of a courtier' should be 'rather something grave and sober than garish…a black colour hath a better grace in garments than any other'. Although his message seemed to have only a limited appeal to his fellow-countrymen, it fitted perfectly with attitudes evolving in Spain. The Spanish courtier was grave where the Italian was gay, sober where the other was flighty. He viewed life in the looking-glass of death and his bleak approach eschewed unnecessary and over-elaborate ornamentation. With the growth of Spanish power in the mid-sixteenth century, Spanish

attitudes to dress began to dominate the rest of Europe. Decoration was reduced and gaudy colours became unacceptable. Black took over as the prevailing colour.

It is not known why the Spanish kings preferred black, though Charles V had always been noted for the sobriety of his dress. His successor, Philip II, favoured black to such an extent that it was taken up as the fashionable colour by all upper-class Spaniards.

There are several explanations for its subsequent popularity. Black reminds us of our mortality and in so doing conveys a gravitas lacking in most other colours. Despite its powerful impact, however, it never overshadows the individual. In a century in which humanism was taking hold, it created a neutral but dramatic setting for the face, the visible proof and mirror of the soul.

By the end of the sixteenth century, black had finally come into its own. People who understood fashion realized that it possessed nuances which brought out the richness and variety of surface and texture. They saw that black on black – heavy velvet over thick satin and liquid silk – could be 'colourful'. It had infinite gradations of subtlety and richness which would be destroyed by the addition of strong, bright colour. It was noted also that black gave fine furs a lustre that was often lost when they were used with colour, and that gold, silver and rare stones looked best against a sombre background.

Black was soon favoured all over Europe as the court colour, based on the Spanish model. It became a part of fashion's vocabulary and would move in and out of style, frequently at a very different social level, right up to the present day. But of course not everyone was in love with its sombre subtlety. Despite its being the semi-official colour of power, there were plenty of men who preferred something more exuberant.

All across Europe the early seventeenth century was the age of the fashionables, men for whom dress was all and criticism and ridicule nothing. Precursors of the Bucks, Beaux and Dandies, they were a standard feature of all courts, and met with almost total condemnation for their dedication to all that was most extreme in style.

The fashionables viewed dress in a fundamentally different way from the men of power who have concerned us up to now. Their dress carried no hidden messages and had nothing to do with politics; it was simply and entirely the gratification of narcissism. The fashionables were in love with themselves and their appearance. Strangely sexless, almost hermaphroditic, they contained within themselves sufficient of each sex to be entirely self-satisfied, needing neither men nor women for sexual gratification. Talk of sex – seductions, conquests, even rapes – may well have taken up much of their conversation; pursuit of the opposite sex may have appeared to occupy all their thoughts and much of their day but, in truth, they were acting out a convention. Their hearts belonged to themselves – and their wardrobes – alone.

Exaggerated in pose and appearance, they circled around James I of England and Henry II of France in their dramatic ruffs, their stuffed and quilted doublets and hose, their slashed and embroidered breeches tied with ribbons, and their folded long boots of softest leather. These last were such a craze that the Spanish ambassador told the king of England that he would amaze his countrymen when he reported that 'all London is booted and apparently ready to walk out of town'. The fashionables glittered and jangled with rings, necklaces, chains, earrings, swords, spurs and anything else which might feed their vanity. James, who loved show as much as he did young men, did nothing to check the excesses. As the *Oxford History of England* expresses it, the court of James I was a hotbed of passions and intrigues not helped by the king's 'strange infatuations for favourites chosen for their youth, graceful and handsome figures, and willingness to flatter their master. His habit of

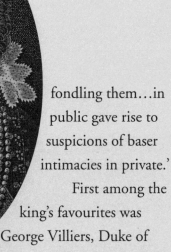

fondling them…in public gave rise to suspicions of baser intimacies in private.'

First among the king's favourites was George Villiers, Duke of Buckingham, irresistibly attractive to both sexes and a man of ruthless and criminal ambition. Vain to the point of madness, he is described in a manuscript in the Harleian collection as appearing at even an ordinary 'dancing' in clothes 'trimmed with great diamond buttons, and to have diamond hatbands, cockades and earrings, to be yoked with great manifold knots of pearl, in short, to be manacled, fettered and imprisoned in jewels'. His appearance must have had all the unreality of an Erté costume design for the Folies-Bergère.

When Villiers went to Paris in 1625 for the proxy marriage of Charles I of England to the French princess Henrietta Maria, he took with him twenty-seven suits of clothes, 'the richest that embroidery, lace, silk, velvet, gold and gems could contribute'. For the actual ceremony he chose one of white uncut velvet 'set all over, both suit and cloak, with diamonds'. Not surprisingly, his dress as much as his affected behaviour made him an international talking point.

Such extravagance was not unique. For the christening of Louis XIII, Marshal de Bassompierre's robes of cloth of gold were trimmed with real pearls. The German general

and diplomat Hans Meinhard von Schönberg left seventy-two richly embroidered and bejewelled suits at his death. Henry, Prince of Wales, brother to Charles I of England, ordered thirty-eight suits – of velvet, satin and silk – in one year alone.

It was a time of swank and prodigality, and every opportunity was taken to play complicated semantic games with clothing. In France, where court life still dominated, the theatre was a passion. In the reign of Louis XIII, the Court Ballets became an obsession, with the king, queen and all their retainers so eager to dress up in the costumes created by Daniel Rabel that sometimes the performance could not take place for the crush of people invading the stage, to see and be seen.

At the English court, masques written by Ben Jonson and staged and designed by Inigo Jones stimulated interest in fashion. In either country, a court gallant cut a remarkably theatrical figure. Fluttering with ribbons the length of his body; be-bowed at every possible point, including shoulders, breast and knees; topped with a periwig which curled, waved and flowed from his large feathered hat; and terminated by his enormous boots with their turned-down tops, he must, when not languidly posing, have looked awkward, jejune and constrained by his extreme fashionability.

It was the boots, more than the lace, ribbons, feathers and bows which marked out the peacock male from his fellows. Edward Grimston in *The Honest Man* says of the young men of the court

The Picture of an English Antick, with a List of his ridiculous Habits, and apish Gestures.

Maids, where are your hearts become ? Look you what here is!

1 His hat in fashion like a close-stoole pan.
2 Set on the top of his noddle like a cox-combe.
3 Banded with a calves tail, and a bunch of riband.
4 A feather in his hat, hanging downe like a Fox taile.
5 Long haire, with ribands tied in it.
6 His face spotted.
7 His beard on the upper lip compassing his mouth.
8 His chin thrust out, singing as he goes.
9 his band lapping over before.
10 Great bandstrings with a ring tied.
11 A long-wasted dubblet unbuttoned half way.
12 Little skirts.
13 His sleeves unbuttoned.
14 In one hand a stick, playing with it, in the other his cloke hanging.

15 His breeches unhooked, ready to drop off.
16 His shirt hanging out.
17 His codpeece open, tied at the top with a great bunch of riband.
18 His belt about his hips.
19 His sword swapping betweene his legs like a Monkeys taile.
20 Many dozens of points at knees.
21 Above the points of either side two bunches of riband of severall colours.
22 Boot-hose tops, tied about the middle of the calfe, as long as a paire of shirt sleeves, double at the ends like a ruffe band.
23 The tops of his boots very large, turned down as low as his spurs.
24 A great paire of spurres, gingling like a Morrice-dancer.
25 The feet of his boots 2 inches too long.
26 Two hornes at each end of his foot, strad-ling as he goes.

that they 'drown half their stature in great boots' and similar complaints by French critics reveal that both the fashion and the criticism were common currency. Most people would have found Tom Brown's description of a Beau, written in 1702, satiric but sympathetic: 'He made a most magnificent figure. His periwig was large enough to have loaded a camel, and he had bestowed upon it at least a bushel of powder, I warrant you.'

There is nothing effete about this swaggering figure. In spirit miles away from the effeminate mince of the fop, his confident stride is directly related to the sinister strut of the Tudor courtier.

Lord Chesterfield pointed out that the difference between a man of sense and a fop is that the fop values himself because of his dress and the man of sense laughs at it. In the second point he is wrong – no man of sense undervalues the power and importance of appearance – but in the first he has surely hit a universal truth. The fop, Macaroni – or whatever other names society has given across the centuries to the over-fashionable man – has been universally assumed to forfeit too much of his masculinity for the lure of the latest style. In literature, his type abounds as something to be mocked and pitied.

Men besotted with their appearance were a standard feature of Restoration comedy. Tottering on stage in high heels, wearing vast petticoat breeches, their voluminous presence was the signal for wit, cynicism and sophistication. Such beribboned beauties, outrageously overdecorated, were condemned by Anthony Wood in 1663 with the comment, 'A strange, effeminate age, when men strive to imitate women in their apparel.'

But fashion was beginning to bow to democracy. No longer the sole pleasure of the rich upper classes, it was increasingly a thing also to be enjoyed by the middle classes, the new upwardly mobile professional men aware of the importance of dress in aiding ambition.

ABOVE: 'The Picture of a English Antick', broadsheet, 18 November 1646

VANITY
AND
OSTENTATION

Nigel Nicolson described Versailles as a 'concentration camp of crystal and gold' but Louis XIV loved it so much that between 1666 and 1715 he spent not one night in Paris, the nominal capital of his country. It was only at Versailles that he felt able to safeguard the myth of the Divine Right of Kings by ruthlessly controlling the thoughts, manners and appearance of all those granted entry to this most artificial of worlds.

French fashion in the reign of Louis XIV was characterized by reckless extravagance, instant response to caprice and an endless striving for magnificence. It ate up fortunes and completely swamped any concepts of good taste that might at one time have been present at the French court. Around the Galerie du Palais, expensive shops catered to the needs of the fashionable. Linen drapers, lace-makers and glovers displayed their wares for a grasping clientele, greedily in love with everything new. Such seductive shops were found in no other city and they gave late-seventeenth-century Paris a unique fashion lead which manifested itself in both 'the purples of pride' and 'the pinks of vanity', as Nicolson puts it. Pride – in one's power, wealth and social position – has always been a valid reason for male display and has often been accepted as a necessity. What Louis XIV made legitimate was vanity. Criticism of vanity has always been inherent in the names given to fashionable men – fop, jackanapes, popinjay, even gallant – but the glory of Versailles made every variety of conceit and narcissism acceptable.

Everything about life at Versailles was ritualized. In his *Mémoires*, Talleyrand writes: 'In place of one class, there were seven or eight – of the Sword, of the Bar, of the Court, of the Provinces, old and new, large and small. Each pretended to be superior to the other, which, in turn, claimed to be equal to the former.' The king kept the loyalty of the aristocracy by honouring some of its members with an exclusive form of dress: the *justaucorps à brevets* – a blue coat lined with scarlet and embroidered in gold. A reward for loyal attendance on the king's person, it was originally granted to fewer than thirty of the many hundreds of aristocrats who thronged through Versailles, but eventually the number entitled to wear it was fixed at fifty. Today such a uniform would be seen as the mark of servitude it surely was, but at Versailles the highest in the land competed for the honour of wearing it.

Our modern visualization of the Sun King is of a man weighed down with expensive and extravagant clothing; an effete and even slightly effeminate figure, with somewhat unhealthy interests. Nothing could be further from the truth. Louis XIV was a megalomaniac – and a robust one at that. He had all the vigour of a man convinced that his God-given role was to safeguard the continuity of the Divine Right. And, far from spending all his time following the pursuits of the indoor life – dalliance, flirtation, dancing and feasting – he hunted virtually every day of his life.

He was, of course, the most magnificently dressed man in Europe – indeed, in the world. Profligate, cynical and manipulative he may have been, but he always looked the picture of majesty. According to Diana de Marly's *Louis XIV and Versailles* (1987), he wore for his coronation at the age of fifteen 'a tunic of violet satin and a black velvet toque garnished with white ostrich plumes and a double aigrette'. His shoes, heavily gold-embroidered, were of lilac velvet. John Evelyn describes Louis in his diaries as 'like a young Apollo' in a suit that was so heavily and richly embroidered that it was impossible to see the fabric underneath. To meet the Turkish envoy in 1669, Louis wore a coat literally covered with diamonds, which was said to have cost 14 million livres.

RIGHT: Louis XIV, the Sun King, dressed as Apollo, God of the Sun. Drawing by Henry Gissey

Louis influenced kings and courtiers across Europe. Charles II was so enamoured of French fashion that he had his coronation clothes created and cut by Sourceau in Paris, and merely finished by his London tailors, John Allen and William Watts. In the Netherlands, the Prince de Ligne was deputed to visit London on behalf of Philip IV. The extravagant suits to be worn on the visit by the prince and his son did not come, as might have been expected, from Brussels, or even Spain – until recently the arbiter of taste in stylish dress for the whole of Europe – but from Paris.

At Versailles the demands of style went beyond clothes. In such a heavily ritualized and uncomfortably formal world, everything was part of the fashion. How to enter a room, make a bow, escort a lady – even just how to walk, stand or sit to advantage – were all of vital importance. The way one moved – affected as it was by the cut and material of one's clothes – was considered to be a surefire indicator not only of class but also of style.

Even when people were banished from this glittering world, its rulings still held sway. The Comte de Gramont, notorious gambler and man of pleasure whose licentiousness was legendary even in Versailles, had the misfortune to fall in love with Mademoiselle de la Motte Houdancourt, one of the Sun King's mistresses. Exiled for this indiscretion, he arrived in 1662 in London, where he became such a social sensation that it was necessary to issue him with invitations to dinner eight or ten days in advance – a

practice unheard of at the time. Happy though he was in Whitehall and Windsor circles, it was still to Paris that he looked for everything to do with his appearance. A courier was dispatched every week to bring back a suit of the correct French cut and, in addition, certain 'menues denrées d'amour', such as perfumed gloves, small vanity mirrors and beauty essences.

Heterosexual, irreligious, immoral, and often dishonest and vindictive, Gramont was typical of the new man of European fashion. He could have been at home in the sub-sect which appeared in France halfway through the seventeenth century: the Petits-Maîtres, a group of highly fashionable nobles renowned for debauchery. Obsessively concerned with the minutiae of their appearance, walking monuments of affectation, they are part of the whispering, gossipy world so brilliantly captured by Pierre Choderlos de Laclos in *Les Liaisons dangereuses* (1782) – a world of intrigue, flattery, flirtation and, ultimately, corruption.

And they dressed the part, in heightened versions of the current fashion. They wore their wigs just a little taller than those of the rest; their red heels – which, in deference to Louis XIV, who had introduced them, were adopted by everyone at court – were just a trifle higher than normal; their coats fractionally more tightly waisted and fuller skirted. But nothing about their appearance was so exaggerated as to invite ridicule. And though they hid their dissolute attitudes behind a smokescreen of exquisite manners, this could not entirely disguise the fact that they were libertines. It was this characteristic as much as their dress which led to their being copied a few years later by young men from the middle classes.

In the copying, however, the formal, artificial elegance of the original became baroquely extreme. The moment the movement began to appeal to the bourgeois it lost its aristocratic éclat. The version of the Petits-Maîtres that has come down to us today is, in fact, that of these lesser second-stringers with their extravagantly overblown wigs (often coloured bright red) and ridiculously high heels. Everything about their appearance was a parody of upper-class

The Macaroni Painter, anonymous, *c.* 1800

decadence. Whereas the original Petits-Maîtres had dressed in order to make a fashion statement, the statement the bourgeois Petits-Maîtres were making was a political one. Their appearance – and their exaggerated pantomime gestures – were a way of showing contempt for the upper class. In fact, these neo-Petits-Maîtres, anti-aristocracy and anti-monarchy, were the precursors of the coming Revolution and their link with the extravagantly dressed young dissolutes of post-Revolutionary France is obvious.

Fifty years later, London's answer to the Petits-Maîtres was the Macaronis, a collection of insiders who deliberately placed themselves outside and in conflict with the established order and dressed in a way that not only showed their alienation but was perfectly calculated to incense traditionalists.

The Macaronis were in fact the first political movement of the young against the old using clothes as a weapon. The very name was an act of aggression – to choose an Italian food which had none of the solid associations of 'the roast beef of old England' was guaranteed to insult the Establishment who, unlike most of the population of Britain at that time, actually knew what macaroni was, and could be relied upon to dislike it as slippery, unreliable and unsatisfactory – in fact, to their minds, thoroughly Italian. The name had other nuances, too. Long before Byron, Italy was known among sophisticated men as the home of unnatural practices, including sodomy. The authorities in most major

Italian cities turned a blind eye to these practices, certainly in those cities which foreign travellers might frequent in order to gratify lusts other than that of learning about an ancient civilization. For a group of iconoclastic young men to select such a name was a confident way to commence battle.

But the name was not their primary weapon. What chiefly shook up their elders was that the Macaronis took fashionable male dress of the time and pushed it over the edge by exaggerating and distorting it so that its truly feminine basis was clearly visible. The Macaronis wore the fashionable lace – but wore too much of it; they chose satin and silk – but at its shiniest; in an era when the male hat – large, cocked and feathered – had become more a sexual symbol than a head covering, they chose a tiny version of it which they actually wore; at a time when wigs were becoming simpler, they piled theirs to rococo heights. Every item of dress was carefully selected to guy the accepted male style. And in a period when even walking and standing were matters of artifice, to be taught by dancing masters, they adopted a mincing gait which was a pastiche of the silliest of female walks.

The effect was to dismay, alarm and alienate. Many theories have been put forward to explain what has been termed the Great Masculine Renunciation, when men turned their backs on decorative and complicated dress. Many of them are persuasive. But nothing kills a fashion – especially for men – as effectively as ridicule.

The Macaronis highlighted the fact that extravagance was ridiculous and conspicuous consumption vulgar, and that both were open to the charge of effeminacy. The effect of this was to drive underground all the show and swank previously given to clothes. Consumption became more discreet and, for upper-class men, fashion became a more circumspect, almost secret, pleasure. Ingenious nuances of cut, fit and proportion began to replace the extravagance of decoration. From now on gentlemen would communicate with one another through the subtleties of tailoring, in a language that would seem not merely foreign but totally incomprehensible to those who were not gentlemen.

The Macaronis dealt the first hammer blow to the male as visual peacock, but their political role was equally important. The astute statesman Charles James Fox – slovenly, anti-Royalist champion of the people – dressed in Macaroni fashion at a time when to do so was a clear political gesture. By so doing, he highlighted what he saw as the effete self-aggrandizement of the monarchy and the aristocracy. He was only too aware that Macaroni dress would be a goad to his political opponents – not least the red high heels which he knew to be an obvious badge of the servility of courtiership at Versailles. He wore them as a warning and a challenge.

The most obvious reaction against all the mincing and posturing of the Macaronis was the birth of the Buck – the barrow boy of the aristocratic classes who heralded the beginning of the nineteenth century. Before he made his appearance, however, the French Revolution swept away the most pampered and pernicious court in Europe – and, with it, the dress codes that had played such an essential role in its stability. Paradoxically, the Revolution also used clothes as a political tool. Even before the Revolution proper, when the Estates General was held at Versailles in 1788, the Marquis de Brézé, master of ceremonies, drew up codes which clearly distinguished between the dress of members of the Church, the aristocracy and the professional classes. The First Estate, the clergy, were to attend in ecclesiastical dress; the Second Estate were allowed black silk or cloth coats, gold-trimmed silk breeches, a sword and a feather-trimmed hat. The Third Estate, not being recognized as gentlemen, were confined to black cloth with plain muslin cravats and were not allowed to carry swords. These restrictions caused great resentment.

As the Revolution gathered pace, the formality of French fashion was replaced by a new and practical form of gentleman's dress based on the clothes of the English country gentleman, which had evolved during the early decades of the eighteenth century. This English country look was as sophisticated as any fashionable male dress had ever been – in its rejection of flash, glitter and shine. Certainly, it proclaimed a confidence in class and breeding that required no gilding. The French fell in love with Le Style Anglais. Fashionable argot began to be peppered with English phrases and expletives and the Prince de Ligne could write in despair: 'Horses and gigs will be the ruin of young men in Paris.' French Anglomania was, initially at least, a love affair with the horse and with the freedom it appeared to confer on young bloods of the English aristocracy. English upper-class life had a style, a pace and a raciness that was totally foreign to France. The urge to compete, the will to win and the ability to be a good loser struck a chord in the French upper class, who were worn out by the stultifyingly boring dance around the monarchy which had previously characterized their life. Even before the first shot was fired at the Bastille, French monarchical power was going, sapped by what were perceived as the more relaxed social and political freedoms across the Channel.

And the freedom of Albion was clothed – to French eyes – in an entirely modern way, in keeping with the attitudes of the times. So the Englishman's mannerisms, reflected in the new informality of poses for portraits, were fervently copied, as, too, was his dress – that of the country milord. His riding coat became the French redingote; his boots and well-cut breeches were taken up with such enthusiasm that, though hostesses frowned, they even appeared at smart assemblies and fashionable gatherings in Paris as though their wearer had just that moment returned from the rigours of the chase. It was all seen as the epitome of dégagé good taste,

Culotte & Guêtres de Peau Couleur de Cuir. Canne à Parapluie.

French gentleman dressed in English style, Paris, 1790s. Illustration by Horace Vernet

English-style, and would have marked the end of the frivolity of formality even if the French Revolution had not taken place.

Balzac described 1789 as the time of the great debate between silk and broadcloth, but the debate had really been going on for more than thirty years and broadcloth had triumphed. Elegant understatement was to be the currency of the future. By 1793, the revolution which had earlier seen Jacques-Louis David commissioned to create an egalitarian dress for all was witness to the edict which proclaimed: 'No person from either sex should force any citizen...to dress in a particular fashion...each one is free to wear the dress or accessories of his or her sex as preferred.' It is the last two words which make this such a startlingly modern statement.

First to take advantage of the new relaxation were the Muscadins – the bourgeois supporters of the royalist cause who took their name from the heavy musk with which they perfumed themselves. Out of their extravagance grew the

Incroyables who, in deference to English upper-class speech patterns, preferred to drop the 'r' and be known as 'Inc'oyables'. In fact, their speech was as decadently slipshod as their unkempt appearance. Devotees of the popular singer Garat, they made their speech so guttural and 'Garatized' that it seemed at times like a secret language – as they intended. Whereas the appearance of the Muscadins was based on an amalgam of French taste and the dress of the English gentleman, the dress of the Incroyables looked as if a Macaroni had been dragged through a hedge and then trampled on by his horse. The results did not win universal praise. A female contemporary quoted by Octave Uzanne in *Fashion in Paris* (1898) wrote of them:

> They have adopted a style of dress intended to differ in every detail from that worn by the youthful aristocracy – a very short waistcoat, a coat with broad swallowtails, trousers that would make me a gown, short Russian boots, and a neckcloth in which they are fairly buried. Add to this costume a walking cane like a tiny club, half the length of your arm, an eyeglass the size of a saucer, hair curled into ringlets, falling over the eyes and hiding half the face, and you will have some conception of the Incroyable...

Theatrical in pose and passions as well as in dress, the Incroyables loved excess – their stiff collars were so high that they almost hid the face and gained them the nickname of 'The Invisibles'. But for all their originality, they were no more than a splendidly diverting dead-end. Their dress could take current fashion no further.

Les Incroyables, from the series *Le Bon Genre*, late 18th century

LICENCE
AND
AUTHORITY

The English sporting writer Pierce Egan, whose works proved compulsive reading for fashionable young men-about-town in the early nineteenth century, described the Dandy's pedigree as follows: 'The Dandy', he wrote, 'was got by *Vanity* out of *Affectation* – his dam, *Petit-Maître* or *Macaroni* – his grandam, *Fribble* – his great-grandam, *Bronze* – his great-great-grandam, *Coxcomb* – and his earliest ancestor FOP.'

Egan's heart was with the Bucks or Bloods of the same period who, as their names suggest, were high-spirited young men full of sexual energy. They represent the other side of the Regency coin, a coin wrongly believed to belong both socially and sartorially to the Dandies alone, thanks to the towering figure of George ('Beau') Brummell. For whereas true English Dandies were thin on the ground and virtually invisible outside their chosen terrain (bordered to the north by London's Oxford Street, to the east by Bond Street, to the south by Pall Mall and to the west by Park Lane), the Bucks enjoyed town and country with a zest that would have caused the fastidious Brummell and his companions to shudder. The two groups perfectly exemplify the dichotomy in the lives, aspirations and pleasures of the upper-class English male in the nineteenth century. On the one hand, all is cultured, refined and intellectualized. On the other, life is boisterous, physically demanding and earthy. Of the two, it is the Bucks who have captured the imagination, despite the fact that they never produced a leader in the Brummell mode.

TATTERSALS. *Tom and Bob; looking out for a good-one, among the deep-ones.*

Heavy drinkers and gamblers, the Bucks were essentially sporting men, who dressed like sporting men, in the coachman style. Lord William Lennox describes their attire in *My Recollections* (1878):

> A light drab-coloured cloth coat made full, single-breasted with three tiers of pockets, the skirts reaching to the ankles, a mother of pearl button the size of a crown piece; a waistcoat blue and yellow stripes, each stripe an inch wide; small clothes, corded silk plush made to button over the calf of the leg, with sixteen strings and rosettes to each knee; the boots very short and finished with very broad straps, which hung over the tops and down to the ankle; a hat three inches and a half deep in the crown only, and the same depth in the brim. Each driver wore a large bouquet at the breast.

So arrayed, the counterfeit coachmen would spend hours checking their accoutrements and ensuring that everything about horse and equipage was perfect before racing each other on the public road like nineteenth-century Hell's Angels.

The Buck has been accused of showing 'excessive devotion to stables, dog-kennels and coachmanship' – a failing most would have been happy to acknowledge, since these pursuits, they believed, made the English gentleman – the *country* gentleman – the cynosure of the world. And driving curricles, riding at Newmarket and visiting Tattersall's, the bloodstock auctioneers, were the essence of English life. Add visits to the fencing rooms in St James's Street and the boxing saloon of 'Gentleman' Jackson in Bond Street (the Regency equivalent of a modern gym or health club) and it is apparent that the wealthy and well-bred life of the early-nineteenth-century male was not entirely occupied with posing in the window at White's or gambling all night at Watier's, important as such pastimes were.

But Bucks and Beaux were joined in one respect. For members of the *société choisié*, idleness was essential. Work was highly unfashionable unless, like that of Wellington (always known to his men as 'The Beau'), it was of state. 'Cutting a dash', being 'prime and bang up to the mark' were what mattered – and if you went into debt, you were expected to ensure that it was for a spectacular sum. With individuals losing tens of thousands nightly, this was not so difficult. And when all was lost, there was always the dash to the Continent, usually France, where a ruined Dandy might recover his sheen. A steady stream of defeated and bankrupt men took the packet at Dover, including Brummell himself, who, characteristically, hired his own boat to take him across, regardless of debt collectors snapping at his heels.

Style was everything. 'To live expensive and elegant' was all that was required – apart from birth and breeding, and even these could occasionally be circumvented if you had plenty of the third essential: a great deal of ready money.

In *The Stranger in England*, written in 1807, Christian Goede itemizes the day of a young man of fashion, pointing out that

> of such a one, a single day describes the whole life: he thinks of rising about eleven in the morning and, having taken a slight breakfast, puts on his riding coat and repairs to the stables. Having inspected his horses, asked a hundred questions of his coachmen and grooms, and given as many orders, he either rides on horseback, or in his curricle, attended by two grooms, dashing through all the fashionable streets of Hyde Park…visits the shops of the most noted coachmakers and saddlers…. After bespeaking something or other there, he repairs to Tattersall's where he meets all his friends seriously engaged in studying the pedigree or merits of the horses…or in discussing the invaluable properties of a pointer…drives from one exhibition to the other, stops at the caricature shops and, about three, drives to a fashionable hotel. Here he takes his lunch…and at five strolls home. His toilet he finds prepared and his valet waiting for him…by seven he is dressed and goes to dinner…. At nine he goes to the play, not to see it…but to flirt from box to box, to look at ladies…and to show himself…he then proceeds to one or two routs…about four in the morning, exhausted…he returns home.

Self-indulgent, vain and often fatuous as the young men of fashion were, there was within their number a small group for whom dress and appearance became a total obsession – not an

LEFT: *The Sportsman's Levee*, frontispiece to *Carlton House Magazine*, 1794

exuberant obsession in the Macaroni manner, but one which concerned itself entirely with taste. For this group – the Dandies – extravagance was vulgar, sobriety elegant. The perfection of their turn-out was based precisely on not making a show but rather whispering a statement about confidence and social superiority. Flash and sparkle were left to the vulgarian and nouveau riche. Their leader was George Bryan Brummell, the man whose name has entered history as the creator of the understated look which, even today, is still seen by many to be the archetype of English male dressing.

Brummell's father was secretary to the British Prime Minister Lord North and in 1794, after Eton and Oxford, Brummell obtained a commission in the 10th Hussars, where he became notorious for flouting the rules and honing the wit which had made him popular at university. The colonel-in-chief of his regiment was the Prince of Wales, a man in love with fashion and the fashionable life who fully sympathized when Brummell resigned his commission after three years service because the regiment was to be posted to Manchester. Both men shared the conviction that fashionable life could not be sustained anywhere other than London, with the possible exception of Bath or Brighton. The panache of Brummell's resignation was not lost on the prince; the men became close friends. The prince was entirely in awe of Brummell's appearance and would sit, ensnared,

at the Beau's feet while Brummell dressed himself and prepared his person for its daily appearance in the window of White's (always known as 'the Beau window'). Brummell, of course, loved the fact that his friendship with the prince opened every fashionable door in London.

The Prince of Wales was insecure, hysterical and unnaturally sensitive about his appearance. For his part, Brummell could never allow loyalty to stand in the way of a good witticism. As the prince grew fatter and fatter and Brummell more and more arrogant, it was only a matter of time before there would be a falling out. Brummell had a satirical eye which missed nothing. Moreover, he had fashionable London at his feet and was the arbiter of all things stylish. Why

ABOVE: Anonymous portrait of Beau Brummell from a miniature by John Cooke

should he spare his corpulent friend? And how could the prince possibly affect his standing in society – why, hostesses would prefer Brummell at their tables any day. Brummell was convinced that he could say what he wished. And so he did. His slighting remarks were noted and relayed to every drawing room in Mayfair. In the end, of course, he went too far. A reference to the prince as 'Big Ben', after the nickname of a fat porter at the prince's residence, Carlton House, reached the ears of the heir to the throne. Society's doors began to close. No longer the man to be seen with, Brummell suddenly found that his tailors were insisting that he pay the huge bills he had run up. Furthermore, his gambling debts, previously ignored, began to be called in. By 1816, friendless and hounded by creditors, he was forced to flee to France. He spent the rest of his life in Calais.

Even in exile, however, Brummell remained the arbiter in matters of fashion for all the young men who had eagerly followed his lead. It was his insistence on perfection and his supreme elegance which elevated the Dandy beyond mere vanity and made him, in the words of the historian Arthur Bryant,

> a formidable figure – the wide-brimmed glossy hat, always new; the spotless, white-starched cravat so tight and high that the wearer could scarcely look down or turn his head, and was for ever pulling it up and running his fingers along the bottom of his chin, the exquisitely cut coat worn wide open to display the waistcoat of buff, yellow or rose and the snowy embroidered cambric shirt;

the semi-tight pantaloons or 'inexpressibles', gathered up into a wasp waist and bulging like a succession of petticoats under the stays; the fobs, jewels, chains and spotless gloves; the white thorn cane – a hint of the broad acres that sustained the type – the wonderfully made boots whose shine rivalled the cuirasses of the Life Guards...

And what a fetish surrounded those boots and their blacking. Brummell claimed that his polish was made with the finest champagne – a witticism mercilessly mocked, not only because it was a preposterous lie but also because of the way in which it pinpointed Brummell's affectation for those incapable of appreciating its humour.

But at the outset Brummell had enough status to ride out any number of idiotic pronouncements. And he was helped by the fact that he was the most elegant man in the world, positively exuding what Byron – no mean dresser himself – called 'that certain exquisite propriety'. This is why, for every detractor, Brummell has ten champions, many of whom speak in glowing terms of his uniqueness. 'The grace of his carriage', wrote Virginia Woolf,

> was so astounding.... Everybody looked overdressed or badly dressed – some, indeed, looked positively dirty – beside him. His clothes seemed to melt into each other with the perfection of their cut and the quiet harmony of their colour. Without a single point of emphasis everything was distinguished.... Handsome, heartless and cynical the Beau seemed invulnerable.

But of course he was not. As always, hubris met with nemesis.

LEFT: George Cruikshank, *Portrait of George IV*

Is Brummell to be admired for his outspokenness or are his last suicidal contacts with the prince to be seen as the actions of a man whose conceit destroyed his judgment? Brummell knew that the prince was thin-skinned, and especially sensitive to criticism of his appearance. He knew, too, that his witty remarks at the prince's expense would be all over 'smart' London within hours. Was he so much under the spell of his own publicity that he felt he could not disappoint his public, no matter what the cost?

Clearly, Brummell was an exhibitionist, used to taking risks and expecting his sallies to be rewarded with endless repetition and embellishment. However it is not his wit, but his attitudes to dress, which give him stature and make him a political figure. When Byron placed him second only to Napoleon as a man of importance in Europe (and, rather endearingly, made himself a good third), people laughed, but it was not in fact so far from the truth.

Whatever Brummell was, he was not a fop. There were no trinkets, no bells, about his person. He was neither beribboned nor 'drown'd in lace'. Stiff satins, patches, paint and powder were part of the armoury of the old world, not the new. His appearance was essentially a manifestation of a modern attitude to dress. For him, cut and fit were of the essence. His clothes spoke an insider's language, too refined for ordinary men, and though they set a fashion, they were not new but, rather, the logical continuation of the pared-down elegance of the British aristocrat's country dress, already well-established.

In every part of the world where men dressed in the Western fashion, tailoring had now become all. A Buck might be built like a butcher but the cut of his clothes would pare him down and disguise any crudeness of figure. A Blood might be sloping of shoulder and concave-chested but a good tailor would soon sort that out. Perfect masculine elegance could be supplied: broad shoulders, narrow waist and immaculately figure-conscious pantaloons. The high collar lent stature – and automatically imposed a swanky, arrogant lift to the whole body. The discreet padding to the front of the coat suggested powerful pectoral muscles even where none could be found. The breeches in buff nankeen and silk stockinette, chamois and doeskin not only produced an illusion of nudity, which reflected the period's love of classical statuary, but also enhanced whatever masculinity the wearer might possess by exaggerating his male bulge to such an extent that a lining was often needed to preserve public decency. And if calves were not as powerful or thighs not as muscular as they should be, the remedy was to hand: 'Regarding tight pantaloons in full dress', the cavalry officer author of *The Whole Art of Dress* (1830) wrote,

> though certainly the most proper and becoming in every point of view, yet I would by no means advise any of my readers to assume these without they have at least tolerably good legs. Unless, indeed, they particularly choose to have recourse

to art to supply the defects of a crooked or a thin leg; in which cases a slight degree of stuffing is absolutely requisite, but the greatest care and circumspection should be used.

The Prince of Wales, as well as being obsessed with fashion, also adored uniforms. His whole soul was wrapped up in Hussar saddles, caps, cuirasses and sword belts. He bombarded the leaders of his army with endless modifications to the trim of uniforms. No epaulette, gold braid or feather was safe when he needed something to occupy his mind.

ABOVE: 'The Dandy Taylor', cartoon by George Cruikshank, 1813, showing George IV meddling with uniforms

And yet Pierce Egan wrote that as Prince he dressed 'as plain as the most humble individual in the kingdom'. In *Britons* (1992) Linda Colley points out that

> The British monarchy…up to and after George III's accession, was still powerful but only sporadically splendid and assured and it was George III who began the idea – clearly false – that an English king was just like everybody else. His son continued the deception not only by his manifold weakness and failure of decency but by his dress – 'plain but beautiful'.

Such an approach provided a valuable safety valve after what had happened in France. The British monarchy had taken note of the *Edinburgh Review*'s 1809 comment that 'the diadem of Bonaparte has dimmed the lustre of the ancient crowns of Europe' and all the gentlemen in the land had taken account of Edmund Burke's statement at the time of the Terror that their opposite numbers in France were suffering for 'no other reason than this,

that, without any fault of theirs, they were born gentlemen and men of property'.

As a stabilizing measure in the face of the troubles across the Channel and developments on the other side of the Atlantic, the British invented the cult of the gentleman as hero. Powerful, muscular and educated at one of England's great public schools, his lineaments had to give the lie to Thomas Paine's jibe about the ruling class being a seraglio of males. Heroism, it was accepted, was an upper-class prerogative and though it held little appeal for Beau Brummell (who, like Jane Austen, seems to have been remarkably untouched by the war with France), it was generally felt that great men should dress as near to a heroic ideal as possible – if for no other reason than that women demanded it. The cult of the modern hero was spun round Nelson and Wellington as the perfection of masculinity: the romantic man of action.

OPPOSITE: Jean-Auguste-Dominique Ingres, *Napoleon Bonaparte*, 1804

London Published by W.S. Fores 50 Piccadilly Aug.t g.th 1817

D_d Angelic pon honor-fascinating Creature
monstrous handsome!! D_m me if she isn't
a Divinity!! for further particulars enquire of the Original.

RIGHT: Richard Dighton,
*Portrait of George 'Beau'
Brummell*, 1805

BELOW: William Heath,
'1812, *Or Regency à la Mode*',
1812. George IV corsetted

RIGHT: George Cruikshank,
A Pretty Pair of Pups, 1819

BOTTOM RIGHT: Richard
Dighton, *The Dandy Club*,
1818

OPPOSITE LEFT: George
Cruikshank, *A Fashionable of
1817*, 1817

A pretty pair of Pups.

There are few words more ambivalent than 'dandy'. It can be made to serve a multitude of purposes – praise, blame, even mockery. Its diffuseness reflects the uncertainty of the genre – was the dandy an admirable or a foolish person; was he the high point of masculinity or merely another effeminate fop? The argument still continues, almost 200 years after the type first appeared in Regency London.

About the Dandies' leader, however, there is no doubt. George 'Beau' Brummell is accepted by all as the archetypal figure. Dedicated entirely to the minutiae of dress, Brummell set the highest standards. He believed in fine linen, well washed, and an appearance which was perfect yet understated. 'If John Bull turns to look after you', he wrote, 'you are not well dressed.' Legend has it that his 'fat friend', George IV, was reduced almost to despair by his own inability to match the Beau's perfection. Brummell's ideas dominated male dress in the Regency period and have had a lasting influence. It is possible to make the case that masculine formal dress of today is directly his responsibility.

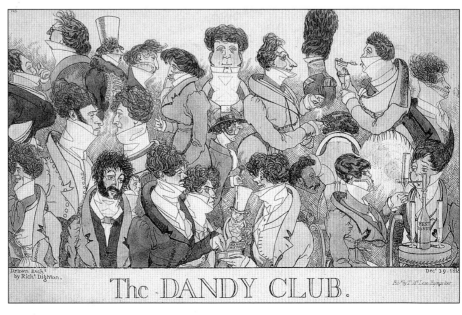

The DANDY CLUB.

VESTED INTEREST

The vest – the seventeenth-century term for a waistcoat, still in use by tailors today and, of course, current in the U.S. – was an essential component of formal dress until the mid-twentieth century. Even in our unbuttoned days, there are occasions when it would be inconceivable to appear without its formalizing influence: with a morning suit, for example. It was first noticed by Samuel Pepys in 1666, when he wrote in his diary: 'This day the King begins to put on his vest…', although, like most seventeenth-century male fashion, the style originated in France. At that point a knee-length garment, it shortened over the years and by the nineteenth century was fixed at waist level, where it has remained. Today, vests – like ties – are often the sole opportunity men feel they have to show their personalities when formally dressed. Colourful materials, exotic patterns and 'jokey' themes are frequently the only form of exhibitionism the modern male will indulge in. Knowing this, designers keen to attract a young market borrow themes and materials from women's dress, children's cartoons and surrealist fantasies to produce something eye-catching and amusing which will enliven an otherwise classic look.

THIS PAGE,
BACKGROUND PICTURE:
Gentleman of fashion, Paris,
1790

ABOVE RIGHT: Tom Gilbey,
1993–94

OPPOSITE, MAIN
PICTURE: Moschino, 1993–94

OPPOSITE, LEFT TO
RIGHT: Hermes, 1992–93;
Jean Paul Gaultier party, 1988;
Byblos, 1992–93

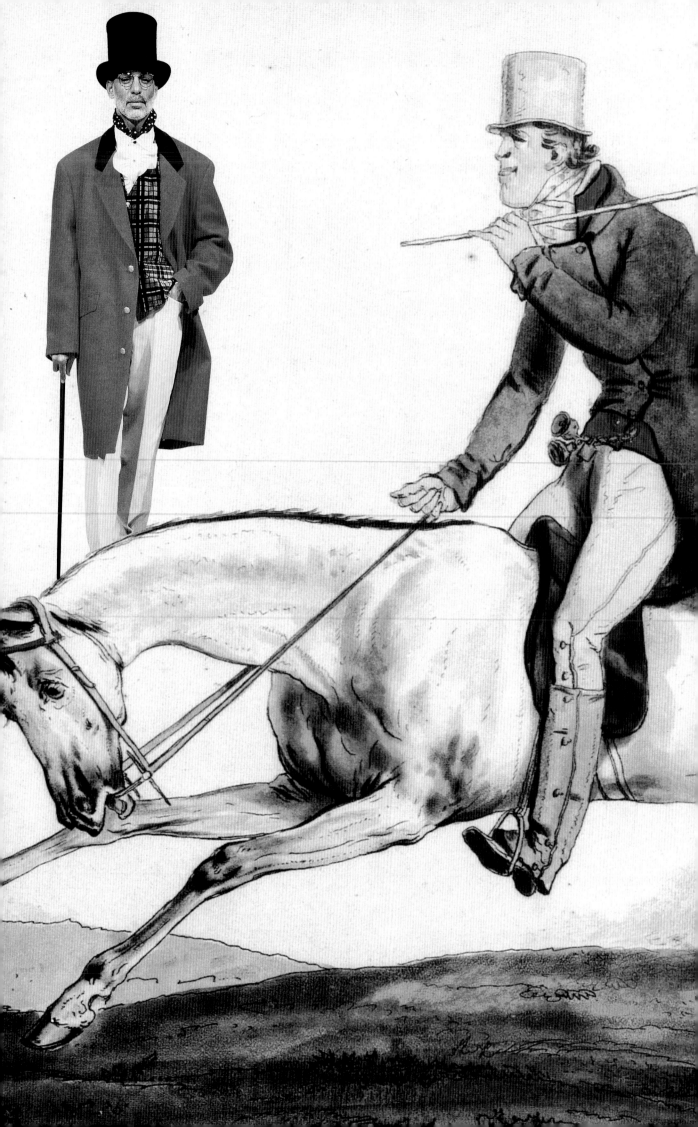

THE PERFECT
GENTLEMAN

As a style-maker and arbiter of taste, the English gentleman has been surpassed in the twentieth century by Italian brio and the elegance of American functionalism, but for almost 200 years his dress alone set the standard for all nations. It was based on the Englishman's traditional love of country pursuits, and since he followed these in all manner of inclement weather, every item had to be practical and utilitarian. From such prosaic requirements grew not only a form of dressing but also an attitude of mind which, even today, distinguishes male and female reactions to fashion. Whereas women feel that they should follow the latest styles, men view even the slightest change with suspicion tinged with alarm.

Quite the most important component of country dress was the stout woollen riding coat. It had to be tough and hardwearing, and because its design was based so totally on its function it quickly evolved as a classic, showing English tailoring skills at their best. High-collared, tailored to the waist and with its skirts generous enough to be unconstraining when the wearer was riding, it crossed the Channel as the redingote. The Duc de la Rochefoucauld described it as 'but a plain coat of cloth with nothing sumptuous about it', and it became the model for the nineteenth-century formal frock coat, still worn by businessmen even as late as the First World War.

OPPOSITE ABOVE LEFT: Daniel Hechter, 1993

MAIN PICTURE: Horace Vernet, *English Horseman*, 1850

ABOVE RIGHT: John Singer Sargent, *Lord Ribblesdale*, 1902

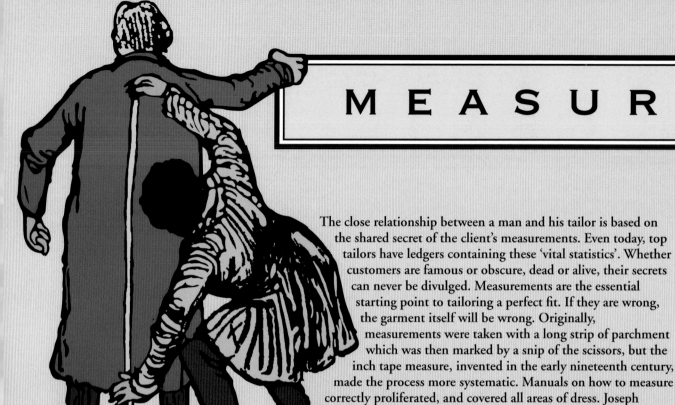

The close relationship between a man and his tailor is based on the shared secret of the client's measurements. Even today, top tailors have ledgers containing these 'vital statistics'. Whether customers are famous or obscure, dead or alive, their secrets can never be divulged. Measurements are the essential starting point to tailoring a perfect fit. If they are wrong, the garment itself will be wrong. Originally, measurements were taken with a long strip of parchment which was then marked by a snip of the scissors, but the inch tape measure, invented in the early nineteenth century, made the process more systematic. Manuals on how to measure correctly proliferated, and covered all areas of dress. Joseph Mainwaring's system, published in 1836, gave instructions on how to 'measure a gentleman for worsted stocking breeches': 'First, lay the end of your measure up at the hip bone… second, measure the thigh very tight, and likewise measure tight the hollow of the knee…' – which is all that is needed to make the perfect fit for the fashion feel of the moment.

Nº II

TOP: From Louis Hverd, *Physiologie du Tailleur*, 1847

ABOVE: From Joseph Coutts, *A Practical Guide for the Tailor*, 1848

OPPOSITE TOP: 'Jerry in Training for a Swell', illustration by George Cruikshank for Pierce Egan, *Life in London*, 1821

OPPOSITE BOTTOM: From George Walker, *The Tailor's Masterpiece*, 1838

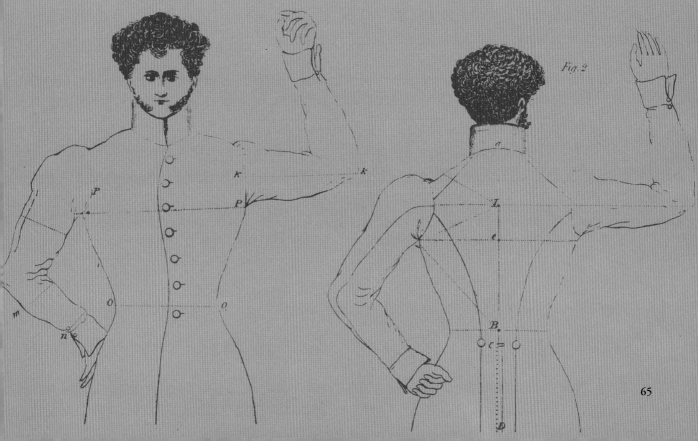

Fig. 2

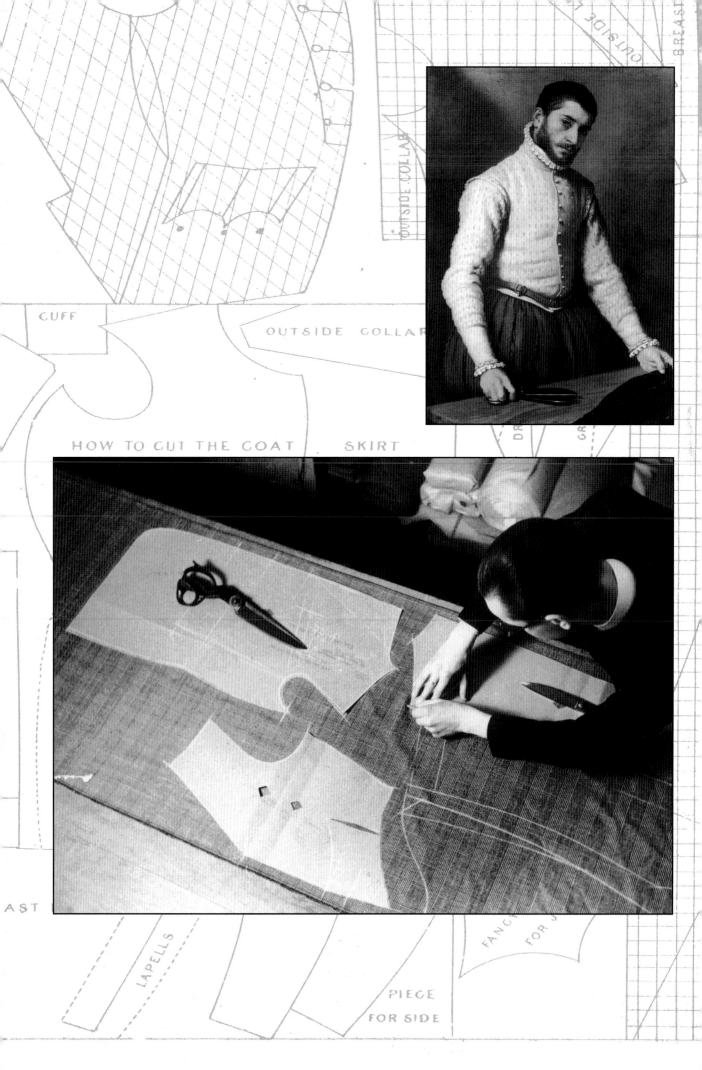

THE ART OF CUTTING

The importance of the craft of tailoring was recognized very early. In 1293 the guild of 'Tailleurs de Robes' was founded in Paris. In the days when fabrics were rich and costly, the role of the cutter was crucial. He began his task by creating a pattern to the measurements of the client. This consisted of flat shapes of the body – arms, torso, etc. – and was originally made out of fabric. Later, the paper pattern known to us today became the norm. Laying the pattern on the material, the cutter traced around it with chalk before picking up his shears. A good cutter required years of practice and experience before he became a master tailor, but if he did he could aim to emulate the career of the early-nineteenth-century London tailor George Stultz, who was estimated to earn more than £40,000 a year – and this despite the fact that a tailor's customers were traditionally so unwilling to pay their bills that, when they did, it was taken as a sign that he had lost their custom.

The classic account of the cutter's role was written by François de Garsault in 1796 for the *Dictionnaire des Arts et Métiers*. The nineteenth century saw this skill raised to an art form. Many tailors wrote books explaining their approach, the most famous being Edward Giles's *West End System of Cutting for the Trade*, which became the bible for tailors throughout Britain and North America.

TOP: Scissors: From Louis Hverd, *Physiologie du Tailleur*, 1847

OPPOSITE TOP: Giambattista Moroni, *The Tailor*, 1546–78

REMAINING PICTURES: The Making of a Savile Row Suit, 1939

BACKGROUND: From Joseph Coutts, *A Practical Guide for the Tailor*, 1848

MILITARY STYLE

Frederick Gustavus Burnaby, who became famous seven years after this picture was painted for his audacious journeys on horseback through Russian Asia, is depicted here by Tissot in 1870 as a male fashion plate, resplendent in the authority of his dress uniform, lolling elegantly at his ease. This is archetypal male flamboyance – controlled, understated but unmistakable – using flashes of gilding and colour to enhance and flatter the shape and proportions of the man. In the military, an impressive sartorial presence was essential in both officers and men to promote the *esprit de corps* on which loyalty and discipline were based. And it is this ability to create camaraderie which gave military dress uniform its appeal in the pop world of the swinging sixties, when Carnaby Street shops like I Was Lord Kitchener's Valet did a roaring trade selling uniforms to the young. But, as Jimi Hendrix's fascination with uniform shows, military splendour can also be used to undermine the very authority it was originally created to instill – it depends entirely on the way it is worn.

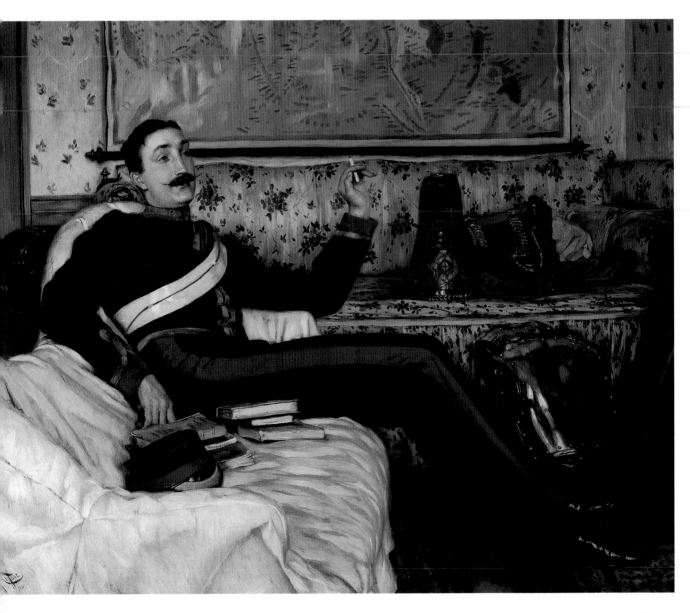

ABOVE: James Tissot, *Portrait of Captain Frederick Gustavus Burnaby*, 1870

OPPOSITE: Jimi Hendrix, 1967

LOUNGE LIZARD

How to dress when relaxing at home was a problem for men in the nineteenth century when daywear was stiff and formal. It was resolved by the birth of the smoking jacket. Comfortable and informal, tied only with a sash at the waist, this was little more than a cut-down dressing gown. Oscar Wilde's is no exception. His collar and cuffs are, perhaps, a little more extravagant than most men would consider reputable, but he has avoided the worst excesses of frogging and piping sported by many smoking jackets of the time. Although his jacket was regulation, his pantaloons and pumps would not appeal to the average nineteenth-century male, who would feel happier lounging at home in the dress favoured by the artist Gustave Doré, whose pose sums up the superior ennui which the Victorian paterfamilias set out to promote as his image.

Modern smoking jackets are remarkably unchanged in appearance, though most men today would feel more at ease wearing jersey sweats.

HEROIC STANCES

In 1845, Comte d'Orsay – a man hailed in both France and England as the natural and only successor to Beau Brummell – was described by the *New Monthly Magazine* as 'the arbiter elegantiarum' reigning supreme in all matters of taste and fashion. In fact, he was more than that. He had a romanticism entirely lacking in the bourgeois Brummell – a romanticism helped both by his stature and his lack of formality. Whereas the Beau was never seen without his coat primly buttoned, the count almost invariably threw *his* coat back from his chest to display a dazzling front, as well as allowing it to slip away from his shoulders in a way revived by high-fashion models in the 1950s. His towering frame was not tightly packaged like the Beau's. He was as impossible to miss for his height and presence as much as for the clothes he wore so flamboyantly.

When Jane Welsh Carlyle met D'Orsay in 1859 she thought him a handsome man but 'of no sex' – an impression no doubt aided by the fantastical finery of his dress: 'sky-blue satin cravat, yards of gold chain, with white French gloves . . . invisible inexpressibles, skin-coloured

OPPOSITE: English Uniforms, 1821–22

and fitting like a glove'. Such exuberance would have appalled Brummell. Jane Carlyle wrote of D'Orsay again in 1845, when his dress – 'black satin cravat, a brown velvet waistcoat, a brown coat . . . lined with velvet . . . black trousers' – reflected the new romanticism sweeping France, and she admitted, 'Well that man understood his trade; if it be but that of a dandy, nobody can deny that he is a perfect master of it.' The painter Benjamin Haydon was impressed: 'such a dress . . . white greatcoat, blue satin cravat . . . hat of the primest curve . . . gloves scented with eau de Cologne, or eau de jasmine, primrose in tint, skin in tightness'. Only Lady Holland, a literary hostess, famed for her 'salons' at Holland House, London, could find no good word for his attire: 'a costume that men disapprove as effeminate'.

Where Brummell was feared for his waspish tongue, D'Orsay was loved. Disraeli found him 'the best and kindest of men'; William Charles Macready claimed that 'No one who knew him . . . could help loving him'; Tennyson declared him a friend and Dickens referred to his 'gentle heart even a world of fashion left unspoiled'. As R.R. Madden has pointed out, D'Orsay attracted men with the mixture of the 'strong energy of a nobly constituted man . . . with the gentleness. . . and tenderness of a woman's nature'. Beneath his extravagance, he was effeminate. Behind his charm for the ladies lurked a hint of androgyny, even bisexuality, which caused Thackeray to agree with the painter John Leech's comment that D'Orsay was not 'a regular gentleman'. Add his

debts, his strangely convoluted relationship with Lady Blessington, whose daughter he married, and with whose husband he might have had an affair, and you have the makings of a much more interesting man than the Beau.

In addition, D'Orsay was not only a dresser, he was a writer and, most important of all in France, he was an artist – and a swaggeringly confident one at that. Brummell thought it vulgar if one's dress caused heads to turn; D'Orsay was piqued when they did not – a rare occurrence, by all accounts. His appearance presented a last bold flash of colour before the heavy duty of being a Victorian high-principled man stilled the fizz of the peacock male. For a time, at least, conformity had become socially, politically and sexually expedient. Everybody wanted to be a 'gentleman' but the ground rules of gentlemanly conduct were dangerously amorphous and subject to unheralded change. Little books of etiquette, small enough to be discreetly consulted and equally as discreetly tucked into a pocket afterwards without spoiling the line of one's coat, poured off the presses. Always anonymous – usually purporting to be by a 'gentleman', an 'officer' or even a 'peer of the realm' – they were produced by the middle class for the middle class. And they saved many a man from embarrassment. The advice was tediously middle-of-the-road and non-confrontational, guaranteed to make nonentities of all who followed it. 'Don't draw attention to yourself and you'll be all right,' is the general tone, but it all seems hideously mealy-mouthed to modern eyes.

All these small manuals have one thing in common: a Sunday-school piety which attempts to make virtues of caution and mediocrity of spirit. No wonder the men who turned to them remained so uncertain and, one suspects, climbed the social ladder slowly, if at all. But other social aids existed which were more reliable and infinitely more entertaining than etiquette books. The popular 'silver fork' novels, a genre which has not withstood the test of time, exerted considerable social influence. Whereas the novels of Lytton and Disraeli were largely aimed at men who considered themselves to be gentlemen, the silver fork novels were DIY manuals for men who were not gentlemen but who wished to be

accepted as such. Characters and situations were used to demonstrate correct and incorrect behaviour. Although their heyday was the first half of the century, these novels were read by social aspirants for many years after. Hazlitt despised the genre, which he dubbed 'The Dandy School' of literature, but the public adored it.

In *Sartor Resartus* (1836), his discourse on the philosophy of clothes, Thomas Carlyle castigated men who believed that their social status came from their dress. His famous dictum that 'A dandy is a clothes-wearing Man, a Man whose trade, office and existence consists in the wearing of clothes' is the railing of the unfashionable man against the fashionable. Like Hazlitt, who criticized fashion as being 'the abortive issue of vain ostentation and exclusive egotism…tied to no rule, and bound to conform to every whim of the minute', Carlyle was convinced that men spent too much time, money and effort on their appearance. The most interesting thing about *Sartor Resartus*, however, is that it should have been written at all. The fact that it was shows how central a preoccupation dress and its nuances had become in the nineteenth century. It would be inconceivable today that a man of Carlyle's stature would devote a book to philosophical considerations initiated by thoughts of dress. A twentieth-century equivalent, the philosopher Bertrand Russell, confined his views on fashion to his comment on the politician Anthony Eden, of whom he remarked, 'Not a gentleman: dresses too well.'

In France, where the subject of dress had always been taken seriously, writers and philosophers were also exercised about the question of how to view the 'clothes-wearing Man'. Baudelaire, in *The Painter of Modern Life* (1863), took as the starting point for his investigation of dress the life and work of Constantine Guys, the artist who, more than any other in the nineteenth century, captured the frenetic elegance – and coarse undertones – of fashionable life in Paris. His chapter on 'The Dandy', a classic of controlled assessment, is based on the belief, which this writer shares, that dandyism has nothing to do with 'immoderate taste for dress and material elegance' but is 'a cult of one's self'. As he points out, whatever dandies are called – Exquisites, Beaux or Lions – 'they all spring from the same origin; they all partake of the same character of opposition and revolt . . . Dandyism is the last splendour of heroism.' Only in France could an intellectual write about dress and fashion with such ringing conviction.

But male dress in the nineteenth century was by no means only an intellectual subject. As it has always been, it clothed not just bodies but attitudes to bodies. It was, in short, about sex. In *Ten Thousand a Year*, the story of a draper's assistant who comes into a fortune, written by Samuel Warren in 1839, one of the characters is described as being 'uncommonly well dressed. What trousers! They stuck so natural to him, he might have been born in them.' Exactly forty years later, George Meredith's novel *The Egoist* was published, the tale of Sir Willoughby Patterne, rich and famous but 'fatuously conceited', who, according to a female neighbour, is popular with both sexes because, 'You see, he has a leg.' Meredith adds to this: 'Well, footmen and courtiers and Scottish highlanders, and the corps de ballet, draymen, too, have legs…but what are they?…simply legs for legwork, dumb as the brutes. Our cavalier's is the poetic leg.'

Legs were not only an indicator of class – the aristocratic ones being long and elegant and, if *Punch* is to be believed, those of the rest invariably short and stubby – they were invested with even greater symbolism. The long leg came almost to be equated with moral probity, decency, worthiness and reliability whereas the lower-class leg denoted the opposite. A would-be politician and leader of men found that a long leg immeasurably improved his stature in every sense.

But, above all, legs were the chief male erogenous zone for nineteenth-century women. Cut-away coats with wasp-waists, padded vests, even top hats, all contributed to the look of streamlined athleticism which remained an essential of upper-class masculine dress for almost half a century. Smooth, worldly and assured of their privileged place in the social order, 'men-about-town' with their arrogant posturing were a carefully contrived and extremely potent sex symbol which the contempt they frequently

showed both for the opposite sex and for the less physically and materially fortunate members of their own did nothing to reduce.

There was nothing flighty about their clothes, just as there was nothing flighty about their top-hatted persons. A wag once said that the top hat was conceived so that an English gentleman would never do anything as undignified as run. He was right. The top hat, like the medieval poulaine, was a shining example of the importance of impracticality and inconvenience in status clothes. Uncomfortable, unstable and unflattering, it had only one function, apart from conferring a spurious dignity – to incapacitate the wearer. It slowed down his movements, gave to his demeanour a grave monumentality and was, in all respects, the substitute crown for the head of the commoner. Like the Guardsman's bearskin or the cavalry officer's shako, it automatically commanded respect, though it lacked the extrovert élan of military headwear

which, like every other item of service dress, had enormous influence on nineteenth-century male fashion.

Armies, like war, had for centuries been simultaneously attractive and appalling. There were privations, but there was also glamour and, for many men, the latter won the day. In addition, the old system of mercenaries offered the opportunity to amass great wealth from the spoils of war: booty, loot and ransom. The dark side of this system was the fact that, when the fighting was over, the army was turned away to fend for itself and to starve if it failed to do so. With the institution of standing armies in the seventeenth century, everything changed. The possibility of great wealth – always a slender one for the private soldier – was replaced by regular pay and the provision of food, clothing and healthcare.

Although press-gangs and devious recruiting officers were endemic, 'Going for a soldier' first became an attractive option in the mid-eighteenth century, especially for those on the periphery of society – the transient labourer, the urban drifter, the square peg in the round hole of an increasingly ordered and proscribed social formula. Not least of the attractions was sartorial: the military man was a symphony of scarlet, blue, gold, white and black offset by a shimmering silver sword. In Thomas Hardy's *Far from the Madding Crowd* (1874), who could be in doubt of the outcome of the battle for Bathsheba Everdene's love between faithful Gabriel Oak and

ABOVE: Illustration from *Gentleman's Herald of Fashion*, 1852

the dashingly fascinating heartbreaker Sergeant Troy after the latter's dizzying display with the sword – which so burnished his 'aurora militaris' in Bathsheba's dazzled country eyes that the fact that he was a rogue could not even be contemplated?

No wonder men queued up for the treatment. Those who were undecided were bombarded by recruiting posters such as the one for the King's Dragoon Guards which claimed 'Any young man who is desirous to make a figure in life . . . has now an opportunity of entering that glorious State of Ease and Independence . . . of a Dragoon.' And, as every recruiting officer knew, it was the glamour of dress that was the trump card.

It is easy to see why the soldiery became the dandies of the nineteenth century. The military man, by definition an outsider who stood beyond society and its rules, fascinated both sexes with his louche behaviour and overtly sexual appearance. He was encouraged to be blatantly exhibitionist in both manner and dress. His clothes were styled to highlight his masculinity and the inescapable fact is that the whole impression could be decidedly homo-erotic. The early nineteenth-century paintings of cavalry officers by Robert Dighton are almost pornographic in their voluptuous delineation of rounded buttocks, sleek thighs and wasp-waists. Certainly the common joke that a man would not purchase buckskins unless they were too tight to put on was brought to life by much of the uniform of some of Europe's crack regiments.

Each country jealously noted the uniforms of the next. According to *The Whole Art of Dress*, the French were particularly admired:

Of the French, perhaps, to pay them a just compliment, they are distinguished for their taste and judgment in selection of uniforms, as their army can witness; while they have been copied, in some degree, by almost all the nations around them, among whom I am sorry to name England. The Garde Nationale and Garde Royale present a very splendid appearance.

French military dress was the envy of Europe. Napoleon had, after all, given much thought to the design of uniforms, though even he made mistakes. At the time of the continental blockade against Britain, the traditional indigo dye of French uniforms became difficult to obtain. Because of this, Napoleon ruled that uniforms should be white. But the battle of Eylau against the Russians and Prussians in 1807 changed his mind. Losses on both sides were considerable – 15,000 French and 18,000 allies. The sight of the white uniforms spattered with blood and gore convinced Napoleon that white could maintain its glamour only on the parade ground, not on the battlefield.

France was ahead in military magnificence, but the Prussian army, reorganized in 1808 on the lines of the Russian army, soon became one of the fashion leaders in Europe. Every country apart from Great Britain was busily redesigning parade-ground dress to make it more dazzling, multicoloured and glittering than before. Chests were padded, waists whittled, thighs encased in skintight breeches and calves in shiny leather boots. Then came the trimmings: silver aiguillettes, gold epaulettes, fringing, piping, complicated intertwined sword knots, velvet facings, silver and gold buttons, frogging, lacing, silk lapels and, above all, bearskins, shakoes, crested helmets and waving plumes.

The colours were just as extravagant. Jackets, pelisses and trousers could, it seemed, be any colour under the sun: cherry red, sky blue, brilliant yellow, rich green, crimson, dove grey, indigo: the list is endless. George Washington favoured an eye-catching green scabbard but when even with this his troops frequently failed to recognize him, he added a bright blue sash for good measure.

The weight of all this theatrical grandeur was borne not only by officers but also by the bands and drummers. These were often dressed in reversed colour to those of the rest of the battalion but they could also have much more extravagant uniforms than those of the rankers. In fact, their uniforms were often far more showy and luxurious than all but the most senior officers. Albrecht Adam tells in his *Memoirs of a War Artist* (1812) how easily these over-fashioned drum majors could be mistaken for more prominent personages, or vice versa. 'I observed', he wrote of the French troops under Napoleon at Duna, 'an important individual dressed in a sky-blue coat covered in gold lace, with gold-laced scarlet trousers and wearing a curious hat covered in plumes. Strangest of all was that he kept walking about very near the Emperor who, in common with his retinue, was on foot. Finally I approached an officer. "Tell me", I said, "who is that extraordinary drum major in whom His Majesty is so interested?" "Mon dieu!", cried the officer. "That is Murat, King of Naples."'

What was the significance of all this ostentation and figure-revealing tightness? Why did the military become the sex objects of the nineteenth century? As we have said, it was partly because in many respects they occupied a position which was beyond the control of the rest of society. But it was also because soldiers, especially those of the officer class, represented a dream of heroism at its muscular best; a dream of colour and narcissism which ordinary dress had turned its back on; a dream of sexual blatancy which was so strongly at variance with a society consumed by both prudery and prurience that it could not fail to bring vicarious excitement. In short, they answered all the longings of the nineteenth-century male: the increasingly colourless civilian man of power.

FLYING THE FLAG

In the late nineteenth century, male dress was washed clean of all decoration. Cut and tailoring became the new marks of distinction. By some mysterious process overt personal display had become so much a form of bad taste and deviancy that it was now transferred from the master to the servant, just as it had earlier been transferred from the state to the soldiery. But, before leaving the military and its uniforms entirely, we must turn to America and acknowledge its great contribution to fashion in the nineteenth century and the lead it provided into the twentieth century. For it was in the United States that the first properly fitting ready-to-wear clothing was created. And the catalyst for this development was military need.

Ready-to-wear was not unique to America; ready-made clothes were available in Europe even in the late eighteenth century, but they were inexpensive and badly made – cheap clothes for the poorer classes. America's great contribution was to give ready-mades credibility by concentrating on fit and finish, so removing the stigma attached to them and rendering them suitable for all classes. It was a major step in the democratization of dress. As early as 1827, T.S. Whitmarsh of Boston was advertising 'from 5 to 10,000 Fashionable Ready-made Garments' and by the mid-1830s ready-made clothing was a standard feature of all tailoring establishments.

The move towards properly fitting garments in a variety of styles had been given a

considerable fillip by the United States Army Clothing establishments, initially set up in Philadelphia in 1812 to regulate the use of colour in uniforms. As Claudia B. Kidwell and Margaret C. Christman explain in *Suiting Everyone* (1974),

> Standardized patterns were worked out by the master tailor. Great care was taken to make sure that they were kept regular in size and shape. The first of every 100 or 200 garments were cut from the original pattern and it in turn served as the pattern for the rest of the lot . . . Once cut out, the garment pieces were put into individual packages with the proper number of buttons, padding, lining, facing cloth and thread. These were issued to the 'widows and other meritorious females' of Philadelphia who were paid a stipulated price for making up the garments in their homes.

Although there were inevitable teething troubles over fit, the system worked remarkably successfully. The long-term effect was that men who had become used to wearing well-constructed uniforms were loth to return to more slipshod methods of dress. The army had given them a lasting belief in the importance of appearance and, as is to be expected of a society at least nominally egalitarian, this affected all ranks. In the Old World, of course, the officer class continued to have its clothes, civilian or uniform, tailor-made, so there was no incentive for ready-to-wear manufacturers to make any real attempt to capture that end of the trade. But in the United States, men of all classes were offered a wide range of ready-made clothing even in the early years of the century. Firms founded at that

time lasted well into the twentieth century. Brooks Brothers, for example, opened in New York as a clothing store in 1818 and by 1859 its advertisements could boast of guaranteeing 'superior goods – the best of work – at prices which have ever characterized our establishment'.

Price was clearly important, but by the second half of the nineteenth century shrewder manufacturers were beginning to realize that it was not the only criterion. If 'good and cheap' had previously been the motto, the appeal now was based on the idea that more expensive clothes were better clothes. So was born the concept of quality ready-made. Once again, North America led the way. While the British, superior in bespoke men's tailoring, which was centred on Savile Row, were still perpetuating the belief that a man could only be well dressed if his clothes were uniquely tailored to fit the individuality of his figure, the Americans were just as convinced that good-quality, stylish clothing could be bought off the peg at a fraction of the cost. Though they were, of course, right, Europe – and in particular, Britain – was not

ABOVE: Advertisement for ready-made clothing from G.W. Peabody's, Kingston, New York, c. 1880

ready to listen. There, trust in a class system –
already eroded in America – had yet to be
seriously shaken.

The confidence that made England such a
triumphant world force in the last decades of the
nineteenth century owed much to the Great
Exhibition of 1851. Prince Albert's idea, it was
initially so ridiculed that it almost died through
lack of interest. But the prince managed to turn a
joke into a triumph and the exhibition eventually
caught the public imagination to such an extent
that daily attendance was often in excess of
60,000.

A paean of praise to the benefits of Free
Trade, the Great Exhibition gave even the poorest
visitor a feeling of pride in his nationality and
created a grounding for the assumption of the
upper-class English male that he might dress
entirely as he wished in the certainty that he
would float above all criticism. Not even the
satire of W.S. Gilbert – remarkably savage at
times – could shake the belief that to be an
Englishman was to have reached the peak of
perfection.

Events in France had a different outcome.
The Franco-Prussian war of 1870, with damaging
defeats for the French army culminating in a
capitulation to the Germans, led to revolution in
Paris. Napoleon III was deposed and a republic
declared. The Second Empire's collapse under the
impact of invasion and defeat left the country
demoralized and insecure. As far as the battle for
the male fashion lead was concerned, Paris never

recovered. For the next fifty years Englishmen
were, quite literally, the lords of the earth.

How was English perfection to be clothed?
The answer was as perverse as it was subtle. No
sartorial trumpets, no fashionable fireworks were
necessary – the English suit, tailored with a skill
that defied its apparent modesty, would be
sufficient. And, despite Brummell's preference for
dark-blue coats, the colour of English manhood
was now firmly fixed. If in the country shades of
green and brown were permissible, in town, the
only colour that had any real clout was black.
Nothing else would do except, in certain
circumstances, cream or white for summer. The
suit became the uniform of civilian life. Though
stripped of all its military colour, it performed
the same function as a military uniform: to unify
and discipline a body of men, and to remind
them that loyalty demanded that they should live
up to the high honour of their birth.

But birth was not always all. The late 1870s
saw the first real fashion movement inspired by
the middle classes: the Aesthetic Movement. This
was not about the grandeur of position but about
something much more accessible: the sensitivity
of the artist. Its protagonists were rarely creative
themselves but considered themselves sufficiently
aware to be able to understand and empathize
with the artistic 'agony'. It was a self-conscious
and affected movement which elevated 'culture'
and its appreciation into an art form in itself. In
dress, the Aesthetic Movement eschewed
anything hard or structured, preferring the

But neither Wilde nor the Aesthetic Movement could stop the inexorable rise of Savile Row or check the dominance of its increasingly precise dress codes. These governed the appearance of the late-nineteenth-century upper-class English male from his hat to his shoes. Elegance was seen in the precision of the detailing as well as in the perfection of cut, which was brought to such a fine art that a wrinkle across the back of a coat or a crease caused by a sleeve a millimetre too long were social as well as sartorial solecisms.

In America, as we have seen, things were different. Although not nearly as well tailored as European garments, American off-the-peg clothes were much looser and moved more freely with the body. The informality of the lounge suit appealed especially to young men, a section of

fluidity which creates an 'artistic' line. It was essentially a relaxed form of dressing, with its knee breeches, velvet Norfolk jacket, flat, wide-brimmed hat, turned-down collar and flowing tie. But it was an outfit which enabled its wearer to cut a dash with more vigour than the languid upper-class 'toff'. The Brummell of the movement was Oscar Wilde, whose clothing bore so little relationship to male fashion of the time that it is tempting to read it as nothing more than an entertaining way of gaining notoriety.

When Wilde visited America on his famous lecture tour of 1882, he played up his appearance for all it was worth, dressing so as to give force to his criticism of the rigidity of male clothing. 'Perhaps one of the most difficult things for us to do is to choose a notable and joyous dress for men,' he claimed. These words were alarmingly provocative, given that joy was the last thing the Victorian male associated with his clothes. Wilde went even further, extolling the virtues of 'beautiful colours' and 'drapery' – both alien concepts in the world of men's tailoring.

the market not specifically catered to in either London or Paris. It was a relatively cheap and therefore largely classless piece of clothing. Sears Roebuck, the mail-order company, sold 9,000 suits in a single day in 1896, a figure unheard of for ready-to-wear garments in Europe.

In the 1890s, America's collegiate classes expanded. As more young men went to college and university – in most cases the first in their family to do so – they became a sartorially influential group which spearheaded the move towards clothes specifically aimed at the 'Young Men's' market. And, much more than in the staider fashion worlds across the Atlantic, this market influenced dress for *all* ages in America. Most importantly, as we shall see, it opened the way for sportswear, which was to become the

major force behind fashion change in the twentieth century.

Nevertheless, in the last decade of the nineteenth century, London fashion for the young had entered a colourful phase. Lively young men-about-town were a distinct subspecies who amused and infuriated in about equal measure with their affectations and enthusiasms. They were known by various nicknames. The Swells, a genre found on both sides of the Channel, and increasingly across the Atlantic, adopted a worldly and sophisticated attitude to life and took great care over their appearance, though they were too conformist in dress to be considered trailblazers. Then there was the Masher, with his overcoat almost down to his ankles, his top hat with its brim extravagantly curled up at the sides, his excessively high stiff collar, his monocle, and, above all, his gleaming white spats. The Masher was a familiar feature of the West End, especially after dark. He spent most of the daylight hours sleeping, waking only to dress for the evening's entertainment. He was noteworthy for the fact that he was virtually the last young man who could go through life in total idleness.

Habitué of the music hall, the young man-about-town was a devoted fan of the performer George Leybourne, who appeared nightly impersonating a thoroughly roguish Heavy Swell and extolling the virtues of the dissipated life. Leybourne's smash hit, 'Champagne Charlie', with its chorus of 'Good for any game at night,

The 1890s and 1900s were the last years when dress was a completely accurate signifier of a man's social standing. They were also the last in which one particular person would initiate and sustain a fashion. That person was, of course, Edward VII, who, from his days as Prince of Wales, was the unparalleled trendsetter for men – on the Continent as well as in the country he briefly ruled.

It is easy to see Edward VII as the ultimate upper-class buffoon; none too bright, in love with sensual pleasures, dilatory in his duties (though a meticulous reader of cabinet papers) and opulently self-indulgent. He was all these things. Also, as his grandson Edward VIII pointed out in *A Family Album*, he 'unquestionably had a wider influence on masculine fashions than any member of the Royal Family since George IV'.

boys! So who'll come out and join me in a spree?' seemed the epitome of raffishness to the chaps in the stalls. Even if World War I had not swept away the leisure and freedom which bred these young men, as well as cutting a horrifyingly wide swathe through their numbers, they would have disappeared, tossed aside by the sheer pace of life – a pace imposed increasingly from across the Atlantic. They gave their last splendidly irrelevant performance in the few years before 1914. At a time when slang was chic, new names were constantly being invented to describe these young men. It was as the B'hoys and Nuts (sometimes spelt K'nuts) that they even had their own music-hall song. Sung to wildly enthusiastic audiences by the languid young actor Basil Hallam in a revue called *The Passing Show* at the Palace Theatre, London, the refrain went as follows:

> I'm Gilbert the Filbert, the Nut with a K,
> The pride of Piccadilly, the blasé roué.

ABOVE: The original Champagne Charlie

'Edward VII, Hurrying from London to Paris', *c.* 1890

As early as 1851, when Edward was only ten, Queen Victoria wrote him a letter, authorizing the boy to order his own clothes. But she made a few provisos. 'I must now say', she wrote, 'that we do not wish to control your own tastes and fancies which, on the contrary, we wish you to indulge and develop, but we do expect that you will never wear anything *extravagant* or *slang*, not because we don't like it but because it would prove a want of self-respect and be an offence against decency...' It was advice he took. Edward VII never wore anything that might be called extravagant. Like George IV, he loved military uniform, was a stickler for detail and had all his clothes tailored with the same crisp precision as those of a soldier.

It was Edward who stimulated the belief that Savile Row alone knew how to tailor with the degree of perfection required by a gentleman. This was manifestly untrue: the tailoring found in Paris, Rome, Munich and Madrid was just as good, but, as a monarch who travelled, Edward was the perfect ambassador for the British look. It also helped that he was so fond of mixing with super-rich Americans, such as the Ogden Goelets, who had everything he required in his friends: 'old' money (at least $50 million), a keen interest in yachting and, most importantly, a 'relaxed' house overlooking the Mediterranean where Mrs Goelets, described by the *International Herald Tribune* as 'very charming and as full of tact as a nut is of meat', could turn a blind eye to nocturnal wanderings and keep at

bay 'the English on the Riviera – a very rag-and-bobtail lot, impecunious to a degree'.

But it was to Marienbad that the king regularly returned. His visits there attracted swarms of fashionable young men from cities all over Europe, including Budapest, Vienna and Berlin. Mingling with them were the tailors and outfitters eager to glean the latest fashion intelligence from the king's appearance. So successfully had the press built up his image as a fashion leader, and Savile Row's reputation as the fount of all fashion novelty, that every day, after the king had taken his morning stroll, the wires would hum across Europe with details of the cut and colour of his suit, the curl of his hat brim, even the shade of his socks. The *International Herald Tribune* noticed his fondness for red and reported in 1930 that 'whatever other changes he makes, he invariably wears a red necktie and red socks while, in the afternoon, he always puts a red band around his straw hat. Already, all young dandies are wearing bright red...exactly like the King. The tailors have all put red in their windows.'

Today it is inconceivable that a portly man, well into middle age, could generate such a fuss, but in the early years of the century, kings were considered glamorous because, in a male-dominated society, they were still viewed as fathers of nations, leaders of empires and rulers of men. Their dress was automatically seen as the garb of power and therefore of interest to all men. Furthermore, no matter how reprehensible their personal behaviour might be, kings were respected simply for their position. As far as publicists were concerned, they could do no wrong: 'As worn by the King' or 'the Prince' were surefire sales generators with the middle classes. Even more surprisingly in the case of Edward VII, what this fat, traditional sixty-year-old wore immediately became the fashion for men young enough to be his grandsons, including young men from the working class.

Edward VIII wrote: 'My grandfather's ample frame became unsuited, as he grew older, to open or cut away jackets. Thus, his coat was inevitably the frock-coat, straight and broad and massive.' Despite all the spa-visiting and taking of the waters, Edward VII's girth grew and his double-breasted frock-coat eventually became single-breasted, 'but unobtrusively so, since it was cut in the same way, with double-breasted lapels'. The frock-coat – an eminently respectable garment – was by no means a new fashion. It was, in fact, the link between three centuries – the eighteenth, nineteenth and twentieth, described by W. Macqueen-Pope in *Twenty Shillings to the Pound,* his 1948 memoir of Edwardian life, as the coat for 'monarchs, princes, noblemen, statesmen; for politicians, merchants, bankers, financiers, stockbrokers, doctors, lawyers; for men of science, actor-managers, schoolmasters, master men of all kinds, even down to shopwalkers'. By the beginning of the twentieth century, however, it had become a sterile item of clothing, no longer

part of the continuing fashion picture. Though still worn at ultra-fashionable gatherings, it no longer spoke of style. By the time Edward VII came to the throne, Paris and London had capitulated to America and the frock-coat was already vastly outnumbered by the lounge suit.

It was inevitable that something would eventually sweep away much of the over-dressing, dressing up and dressing for every occasion. And what did it in the end was symbolized by the

ABOVE: By 1860 the frockcoat and top hat were universal. Drawing by Barbosa

motor car. An exciting and compulsive hobby, far more interesting than hanging around a tailor's all day, motoring appealed to the Bertie Wooster generation not only because it heralded a new informality but also because it enabled young men to be alone with women while speeding along at what seemed at the time a daredevil pace.

The other chief reason why dress rules were doomed to fade was pinpointed by Henri Duvernoi in his *Conseils d'un homme chic* (1913): 'Comfort, gentlemen', he wrote, 'is the main thing in male stylishness.' It was a view that had long been held by the German dress reformer, Dr Gustav Jaeger, a firm advocate of what he called 'hygienic' dress. Though viewed initially as a crank, Jaeger was, in fact, remarkably forward-looking. Taking as his slogan Emerson's contention that 'The First Wealth Is Health', he published in 1904 his treatise on Health-Culture, comprising six chapters devoted to clothing and bedding reforms. It was the chapter on underclothing, in which he evolved his Sanitary Woollen System, which was to have the most far-reaching effects, but his comments on masculine dress are remarkably prophetic.

Much of Jaeger's philosophy of dress reads like the tunnel-vision of the fanatic but in his insistence on natural fibres (in his case, wool), loose fit, and dress which answers the dictates of comfort and practicality rather than responding to the demands of fashion, he was well ahead of his time. And he captured the imagination of thinkers, most prominently George Bernard Shaw, who followed Jaeger's precepts throughout his long life. The sculptor Eric Gill reiterated many of Jaeger's attitudes in his books, *Clothes* (1931) and *Trousers and the Most Precious Ornament* (1937), the latter a splendidly quirky appeal to men to throw away their trousers in favour of the 'unbifurcated garment'.

Gill was worried about the effect of tight trousers on man's sexuality. He wrote scathingly of what tailors had done to the penis, berating them for turning it into an organ of drainage rather than of sex. 'It is tucked away and all sideways, dishonoured, neglected, ridiculed and ridiculous – no longer the virile member and man's most precious ornament, but the comic member . . . comic and . . . dirty'. And so it is today. The penis remains the last taboo erogenous zone.

OPPOSITE: The Italian composer Giacomo Puccini (1858-1924)

TWEED

Tweed was first named in the 1830s when a Scottish clerk misread the word 'tweel', the Scottish form of twill, and put a 'd' at the end instead of an 'l'. The fancy wool trade of the Scottish borders was originally based on the black and white checked plaids used by shepherds. These were popular south of the border as travelling wraps for passengers sitting outside on stagecoaches. But the ground-breaking event which made Scottish tweed the dress of all men who spent time in the country came in 1826, when Sir Walter Scott, hearing that the shepherd's check design had been adapted as a trouser cloth, ordered himself a pair. The fashion immediately caught on as a form of upper-class dress and was brought to London by the Scottish-born tailor James Locke, of Covent Garden. It soon spread to artistic and avant-garde members of the middle classes. In fact, the vogue for tweed became so extensive that 'District Checks' were invented, of which the most famous was the 'Glen Urquart', based on the tweed worn by the factors, gamekeepers and tenants of the largest of Scotland's estates, that of the Countess of Seafield. Authenticity became all, and, to this day, Harris Tweed is genuine only if it bears the industry's label. Standards are still jealously guarded and even now most manufacturing processes are controlled by hand and eye rather than by sophisticated computerization.

OPPOSITE: Vivienne Westwood, 1996–97

ABOVE: Basil Rathbone as Sherlock Holmes, from *The Adventures of Sherlock Holmes*, 1939

RIGHT: Rex Harrison as Professor Higgins in *My Fair Lady*, 1964

IN HAT: Victorian man in tweed, *c.* 1860

Showing off always seems less sophisticated away from big cities and centres of civilization where high standards of dress and appearance are more likely to be reached on an everyday basis. Rural working life does not lend itself to immaculate linen and well-pressed wool, which is why country men dress up with such a sense of style when the occasion calls for it. Got up in unaccustomed finery, the three young German men opposite, photographed on their way to a dance, seem full of confidence. Vincenzo Florio, seen below (centre) with his friends, was no peasant, but a wealthy member of Sicilian society and a man obsessed by fashion. Nevertheless, he is trapped in a kind of provincialism, as are the three Hungarian businessmen shown left, photographed in 1916. All look as if they are trying too hard. In the case of Florio and his friends, so many fashion statements are being made that it is hard to decide which is the most important. One suspects that, for them, it is the amazing collars and ties.

ABOVE: Batorkeszi, Hungary, 1916. Photo by André Kertész

BELOW: Vincenzo Florio (centre) and his friends, Sicily, *c.* 1900

OPPOSITE: Three young men going to a dance, Westerwald, Germany, 1914. Photo by August Sander

SAVILE ROW

The world centre of bespoke tailoring is London's Savile Row, an area as much as a thoroughfare, but above all else an attitude of mind. In Savile Row it has always been possible for a gentleman to purchase any article of dress – with the exception of socks and, perhaps, underwear – made expressly for him to his own measurements. For the elegant Englishman prior to the First World War, to go anywhere else for these items – such as abroad – would be as unthinkable as buying them ready-made and 'off-the-peg'. Not only did Savile Row provide the clothes, it also furnished the rules of male dress. What was decreed by its tailors had the force of a Papal Bull until American influences in the 1920s and Italian in the 1950s weakened its power. Savile Row was brought down by the demands of leisure and the need for ease. Starched shirts and top hats may well have been the hallmark of the gentleman at the turn of the century but they were simply too uncomfortable to last. What has survived in Savile Row, however, is quality, which shows itself in the finest natural materials – tweed, flannel and silk – and the minutest attention to detail. That is why, in these ready-to-wear days, Savile Row, though reduced, is still there, catering to those who are wealthy and patient enough to insist on perfect tailoring.

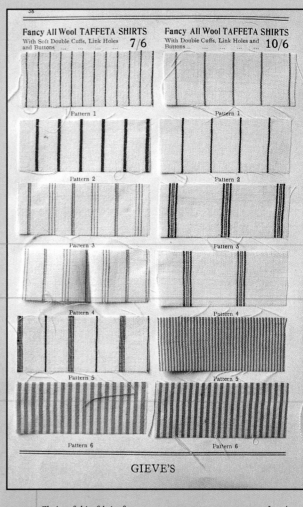

ABOVE: Choice of shirt fabrics from Gieve's original catalogue of 1903

BELOW: View of the establishment of Henry Poole & Co. in Savile Row, c. 1890

OPPOSITE TOP RIGHT: Interior view of Gieves & Hawkes flagship store, No. 1 Savile Row

OPPOSITE: A choice of tweeds at the Bespoke Tailoring Department of Gieves & Hawkes, No. 1 Savile Row

IVY LEAGUE

If Savile Row has always been the touchstone of senior establishment taste, the Ivy League look of the top North American colleges such as Stanford, Yale and Harvard has been the junior version. Essentially youthful and sporty, it has avoided the grown-up, stuffed-shirt quality of its older brother without sacrificing any of its elegance. The future American president Franklin D. Roosevelt, photographed for his yearbook in 1900 in Arrow collar, tie and three-piece suit, epitomizes the look. Relaxed, well-bred, immaculately turned-out but not finicky, this is fashion with which men can identify even today – which is why it is regularly revisited and revised by modern menswear designers such as Ralph Lauren, who rightly see it as a highpoint of American style. What it shows above all is that smartness and good breeding do not need to be stiff and formal any more than being relaxed means a decline into slovenliness. In the aristocracy of male fashion style, Ivy League is as convincingly authoritative as Savile Row and, many would believe, considerably more accessible and attractive.

OPPOSITE: Portrait of Franklin D. Roosevelt, Yearbook photo, Groton School, Massachusetts, 1900

ABOVE: Ralph Lauren, 1996

CENTRE: Logo of Brooks Brothers, New York

BELOW: Advertisement for Arrow collars and shirts, 1913

ARROW COLLARS AND SHIRTS

ARROW Collars are made in the greatest variety of styles and heights, in such a careful way, of such excellent fabrics, that even the most fastidious, to whom cost means nothing, give them preference.
2 for 25 cents

ARROW Shirts fit most men comfortably. They quickly reflect the tendencies of fashion. They do not lose their original freshness of color, and render such sterling service that the label will serve as your guide to shirt satisfaction.

CLUETT, PEABODY & COMPANY, INC., TROY, N. Y. Send for Booklets.

$1.50 and up.

Swagger in male dress is based on the confidence to wear outrageous cut, colour and pattern as if you have just invented them. No dress, apart from military uniform, has given men as much scope as the traditional Highland tartans.

Although many modern tartans were invented by Queen Victoria and Prince Albert as part of their love affair with Scotland, real tartan goes back much further. Conceived as a primitive form of decorative weaving when the skill was still largely in its infancy, and rarely as colourful as we now expect, it was a form of tribal identity, invaluable in war, where it performed an effective job as an early form of camouflage. Today, it is not intended to merge but to stand out in glorious contrast to the drab tones of most male dress. Strictly for extroverts, it is especially attractive to artists and other free-spirited thinkers who enjoy turning themselves into walking works of art.

ABOVE: Picasso at La Californie, 1957. Photo by Lee Miller

TOP LEFT: Basile, 1990

LEFT: Classic Burberry check, dating from the 1920s

CHECKS
AND
TARTANS

ABOVE: Pompeo Batoni, *Colonel William Gordon of Fyvie*, 1766

TOP RIGHT: Paul Smith, 1996

RIGHT: Cattle hand, Dinka tribe, Sudan, 1990

TIES

An exquisite agony of indecision overcomes even the most forceful of men when faced with making a choice of tie. It is easy to see why. Not only is it one of the few items of dress on which a tailor is unlikely to guide and advise – which is why the centre of tie-making in London is not Savile Row but Jermyn Street – but it also offers a dangerous opportunity for extravagance and even theatricality, both of which can easily lead to vulgarity. This is why so many men, even today, opt for regimental and club-based stripes as the safest thing.

In the 1920s and 1930s, when choice was more limited and men more secure, the manner of tying a tie was as strong a fashion indicator as the pattern itself. The large Windsor knot, named after a style first popularized by the Duke of Windsor and originally thought so chic that it was copied by all men-about-town, has since fallen from grace and is now seen as the height of bad taste. Today it is the tie's pattern, colour and texture, rather than the way in which it is knotted, which matters to a man of fashion.

BELOW: The painter Foujita in Paris, 1927

RIGHT: 'A Gentleman Chooses a Tie' by Bernard Boutet de Monvel, from the *Gazette du bon ton*, 1912

BERNARD
B DE MONVEL

VIBRANT VELVET

Of all the rich materials used for male dress in the past, the one that has survived most successfully into the present day is velvet. Rich and subtle, it appeals to the young because it is essentially an informal and non-pompous material. Its antecedents are impeccable: the dress of artists and philosophers, velvet is bohemian, even when used for a formally cut suit. Its appeal to artists lies partly in the fact that it can be produced in a wider and stronger range of colours than those available in more mainstream fabrics. But the real reason for velvet's attraction is that it brings with it remembrances of the decadence of seventeenth-century court life, when it clothed luxury and the joy of sinful pursuits. The most tactile material worn by men, it is the closest thing to exposed human flesh, waiting to be caressed. Since the hippies, velvet has been given even greater informality through the use of patchwork, checks and quilting. This originally home-produced style has been taken up by designers with unfailing antennae for the mood of the moment.

OPPOSITE,
BACKGROUND
PICTURE: John
Rocha, 1996–97

OPPOSITE:
Dolce & Gabbana,
1994

RIGHT: Gucci,
1997–98

HEALTH AND
STRENGTH

The Arrow Shirt man was created in the 1910s by the U.S. fashion artist Joseph Leyendecker. Handsome, manly and brimming with health, the image he projected was in tune with the spontaneity and informality characteristic of the New World without sacrificing any of the elegance of the Old. A sportsman and a winner, he made the Old World Mashers, B'hoys and K'nuts look effete and introspective. Known in his time as a 'hunk of male magnificence', the Arrow Shirt man had a sex appeal that was so direct and uncompromising that the company was inundated with fan mail, including marriage proposals, suicide notes, and poems and songs dedicated to his power and purity from people who thought Leyendecker's drawings were portraits of a real person.

Like his country of origin, the Arrow Shirt man looked outwards and stared the world in the eye, his gaze full of the confidence of the new culture, a culture which needed neither kings nor tradition, protocol nor prohibitions, to give it strength. Twentieth-century man had arrived.

He had not sprung up suddenly, fully formed and without precedent. The antecedents of this new sex symbol can be found in the American West, among men who opened up frontiers, created their own law and order and cultivated the land not only for lordly masters, but also for

OPPOSITE: Eastern dude, USA, c. 1890

themselves. Although there were many sub-species, the model of the Western man-of-action was – and still is – the cowboy.

The psychological and sartorial importance of the cowboy cannot be over-estimated. He gave American men the confidence to be themselves, to follow their own instincts and to eschew any attempts to ape the European – and especially the English – male. After two centuries of looking to the Old World for a lead, American tailors and clothes manufacturers finally found the courage to go their own way. Charles Dickens perfectly captures the new assurance in his description of a New World bootmaker in *American Notes*, of 1842. This 'artist in boots', as Dickens called him, arrives to measure the novelist dressed in formal hat, stiff cravat and gloves:

> [He] walked up to the looking glass; arranged his hair; took off his gloves; slowly produced a measure from the uttermost depths of his coat pocket; and requested me, in a languid tone, to 'unfix' my straps. I complied . . . 'You an't partickler, about this scoop in the heel, I suppose then?' says he: 'we don't foller that here.' . . . he measured me, and made the necessary notes . . . and, taking up the boot again, mused for some time. 'And this,' he said, at last, 'is an English boot, is it? This is a London boot, eh?' He . . . rose . . . put on his hat; drew on his gloves very slowly, and finally walked out. When he had been gone about a minute, the door reopened and his hat and his head reappeared. He looked round the room; and at the boot again, which was still lying on the floor; appeared thoughtful for a minute; and then said, 'Well, good afternoon.'…and that was the end of the interview.

The anonymous bootmaker was an example of the thinking Sinclair Lewis was to describe in 1939 as characterizing the new America: 'no longer a cultural colony of Europe, but a great and adult and individual and slightly lonely nation, that must depend on itself, and that hugely needs to understand the self on which it depends'. The first step on that path was taken by the men of the West. Millions of words have been written about them, most painting a deliberately romanticized picture. Doc' Holliday, Kid Curry, Jesse James and Wyatt Earp are so totally befogged in clouds of heroic male glory that it is now impossible to make any real assessment of their characters. But this is not important. What Americans fell in love with was not the men but the West itself. It was the land which made the men appear so heroic, even as its vastness reminded them how insignificant they were.

It was inevitable that the man of the West would fall in love with himself. The mythologizing of the frontiersman, be he evil gunman, upright lawman, or merely honest cowboy or homesteader, was initiated by the frontiersmen themselves. 'Wild' Bill Hickock, gun-slinger and career gambler, had to wait more than fifty years after his death in 1876 before he was made world famous by Hollywood, but the West's other famous 'Bill' – Buffalo Bill Cody – did the job for himself and opened the door for all the showbusiness 'rhinestone cowboys' to come. He created his road show in 1883 but, even by then, the world he cosmeticized for the theatre

was largely dead. His jaunty hat and extravagantly fringed buckskins would have astonished the earliest cowboys – the Mexican vaqueros on whose dress he had based his costume. And how it must have appeared to the few real cowboys still resisting the barbed wire and railroads which were driving them off the land is easy to imagine.

Novelists like Zane Grey and Owen Wister, who wrote the hugely popular Western novel *The Virginian* in 1902, took an equally romantic view, as did the artists who painted pictures which glorified the West – men like Frederic S. Remington and Charles Marion Russell. Bucking broncos, camp-fire serenades and encounters with Indians were the bedrock of a mythology of heroism based on the lean, fit body of the physical male which was so powerful that it would prove to be the springboard for all the active sportswear of the twentieth century.

What made the cowboy such an icon were the epic feats of stamina and heroism which he was believed to personify. In the early years of the twentieth century he exemplified the restlessness and optimism of America and was a hero with whom the many thousands of refugees from Europe could easily identify.

And his clothes – egalitarian and practical – were totally attainable: though the cowboy himself was increasingly seen as a member of an elite, lesser mortals could at least look the part, something denied them in the countries they had fled.

Three items of Western dress caught the imagination to such an extent that they have survived even to this day, despite the vulgarization and ridicule which they have sometimes had to suffer. The first, the Stetson hat, is as quintessentially American as Coca Cola. Created in 1865 by John B. Stetson, it achieved rapid popularity and became such a fetish item for freedom-loving American males that by 1906 the Stetson factory was producing 4 million hats a year. It had, as Ralph Richmond claimed in *The Stetson Century*, come to symbolize the spirit of the West: 'Not by its six-guns and its saddles, not in its songs and legends does the Old West most truly live in history. It lives in its Stetson.' Millions of Americans would agree, from electioneering politicians (including presidents) to the Big Men of the Big Country – the oil billionaires who see nothing incongruous in wearing a 'Boss of the Plains' stetson with a pin-striped suit. It was, and still is, the headgear of heroes – American style.

Almost as talismanic and certainly more popular worldwide is the cowboy boot, with its decoratively chased leather. In the early days, it was made of tough, hard, unbending hide, since its original function had nothing to do with glamour or smartness but was meant to protect the wearer from the rain and mud, the bites of horses and 'rattlers', and the frosts and bitter winds of the wide plains. Essentially a working boot, it became decorative only after the cowboys had largely deserted the range. By then the 'Cody' factor had cleaned it up, made it shine and paved the way for later showbusiness extravagance. Today, handmade cowboy boots created to a uniquely personal design by craftsmen firms like Lucchese of San Antonio, Texas, Tony Lama of El Paso or the Olsen-Stelzer Boot and Saddlery Company of Henrietta, Oklahoma, are the indulgence of rich fantasists prepared to pay considerable sums for gaudy objects with no real function except display.

Along with extravagant belt buckles, multi-coloured patchwork and embroidered shirts and exotically tooled chaps – the syntax of the modern Country & Western dress movement – today's cowboy boots have nothing to do with the spirit of the working cowboy but everything in common with the hokum of the 'singing cowboys', who were some of the earliest crowd-pullers in film – Gene Autry and Roy Rogers, for example, who brought to the screen the colourful dress of the rodeo world with its heavily beaded vests and fancy footwear.

By the 1930s Western wear was a distinct – and booming – sector of the American clothing industry. At that time the most popular shirt for would-be cowboys was made of brightly coloured printed satin, but showmen went one step further. Chartreuse, fuchsia, sunshine yellow – no colour was too strong and no pattern too intricate to be picked out with pearls, rhinestones or chainstitch embroidery. By the 1950s, kitsch and vulgarity had totally overwhelmed the nobility of the dress of the Old West. In the 1970s, brocade, gold lamé, stretch lurex, ultra-suede and 100 percent polyester, along with flares, bell-bottoms and even medallions signalled the total capitulation of Western wear to show business.

But the third item of Western dress had not lost its way. Denim jeans are as practical today as they were when they first became part of Western clothing more than one hundred years ago. The story of Levi Strauss and his invention is too well known to require repetition. Originally an item of clothing for prospectors and pan-handlers, jeans were not adopted by cowboys until the 1890s. Until that time they preferred striped or checked wool for winter and cotton nankeen for summer. Worn also by farmers, truck drivers and factory workers, jeans took years to acquire their glamour image, a process which began in the 1940s when they changed from blue-collar practicality to college-student nonconformity. It was then that their design and cut were reconsidered for the first time in 100 years. Although baggy working versions continued to be produced, the rag-trade moguls of Seventh Avenue saw that jeans could be made more acceptable as leisure wear if they were cut with greater finesse and more awareness of developments in other areas of fashion. Even so, jeans had a long way to go before they were to achieve their cult status as sexual clothing in the 1980s, with designer labels, fetishistic insistence on 'straight legs' and 'button flies', and fanatical support for a particular brand – archetypally Levi's 501s.

Jeans are North America's great contribution to twentieth-century fashion. Paradoxically, however, they and the whole concept of Western cowboy dress are also anti-fashion. What initially gave jeans their appeal was that they fitted in perfectly with the lure of the West as a masculine territory, where men were nothing if not manly. But the West moves slowly, unaffected by swings of fashion. And this is its great legacy: it destroyed the old concept of fashion for men. As the twentieth century developed and Western

ideas of practicality before show and casualness over formality took hold, fashion interest of the sort shown in Edward VII at Marienbad was seen as effete, unworthy and even sexually suspect. Above all, it was deemed irrelevant to a masculine way of life in which status and display had less to do with the trappings of wealth – costly material, beautifully tailored or expensive hand-made accessories – and more with showing off to best advantage the physically fit body of the active male.

Although the relaxed attitude of the West can, with hindsight, be seen to have articulated the twentieth century for most men because it was so totally in accord with social and political developments taking place at the same time, it went for decades largely unnoticed by the fashion trade itself. Male style magazines, especially *Gentlemen's Quarterly* and *Esquire* from the thirties, make fascinating reading. *Gentlemen's Quarterly*, founded in 1926, was originally a trade publication, though it was later revamped on the *Esquire* model. *Esquire* was first published in 1933, in order to capitalize on the interest in male fashion stimulated by the Prince of Wales. It was not, however, meant to become 'a primer for fops'. Strongly anglophile, it traded in a

ABOVE: Early advertisement for Levi Strauss

fantasy, Cole Porterish world which assumed that all American males were rich, urbane and well-travelled. Just as cinema was an exercise in escapism for the masses, *G.Q.* and *Esquire* were escapism for the classes. The tone was set in an *Esquire* caption of 1935. 'How do we get these fashions?' it asked. The reply – though tongue-in-cheek – was an invitation to snobbery: 'We have observers, trained almost from birth, who practically commute to England where they haunt the very best places and ignore all but the very best people . . .' Beautifully illustrated by fashion artists of the standard of Laurence Fellows and Robert Goodman, the *G.Q.* and *Esquire* ideal of the American gentleman was a strange, composite character, as much British as American, always placed in a gracious, even patrician, setting such as Eden Roc, Cannes, Nassau and St Moritz – places as familiar to the average American's experience as the moon. Although occasions were sporty rather than formal, these illustrations were light years away from those of Leyendecker. The captions were slick, fatuous, snobby and preeningly male chauvinist. In fact, *Esquire* man between the wars managed to personify the worst characteristics of his sex on both sides of the Atlantic.

Both magazines concentrated on creating their own fashion trends but shared a belief in their joint fashion leader. The Prince of Wales, a man whose mind was much exercised by the trivia – even the minutiae – of dress, was a God-given gift to the menswear trade and its

magazines. Even in a country as nominally egalitarian as America, a member of the British Royal family is an unbeatable fashion leader for the middle classes. As Prince and then as King, Edward VIII was obsessed with his appearance – a fact which becomes clear in *Family Album*, an informal book of memoirs he wrote in 1960 itemizing the things which had interested him as prince, king and duke. Of its twelve chapters, three are devoted to fashion, and clothes make a prominent appearance in most of the other nine. For the middle classes on both sides of the Atlantic, Edward VIII's little fashion touches – and he did initiate some new approaches – were something to be watched and copied. Like his grandfather, he even precipitated crazes, though these were, in the long run, insignificant variations on existing sartorial themes.

By the 1930s, however, even if the upper and middle classes looked across the Atlantic to the British court, working-class men in North America were much more inclined to take their role models from more democratic sources. The children of Ellis Island, who had entered the promised land with little more than a bundle of rags, did not want clothes that reminded them of the indifference of kings and the cruelties of religious and political bigotry. Why cling to European decadence when American vitality promised everything to the man of energy? Europe was old; America new. Europe was tired; America was alive with opportunity. Fustian was European – and replete with century's-long associations of peasant persecution – denim was American and democratic.

The first people fully to realize and exploit the new attitudes were neither politicians nor clothing manufacturers, but film-makers.

The cinema, like the old music hall, is an art form which in its early years was deliberately geared to exploiting the attitudes and needs of the lower-middle and working classes. From the outset, it turned its back on traditional cultural models requiring an educated audience. As mass entertainment, it could have no truck with artistic elitism. It was essentially a medium which dealt in characters and situations with which ordinary people could identify. In literary terms, the cinema was creating a Dickensian world rather than the rarefied and narrow spectrum of Henry James. As such, its influence on the attitudes and aspirations of less educated men was immense. It was their looking glass, showing them an image of what they might become. For every man who even noticed a newspaper picture of the Prince of Wales, there were hundreds, even thousands, who wanted to copy the screen appearance of 'working-class' actors like Paul Muni and Edward G. Robinson. When in the 1934 film *It Happened One Night* Clark Gable revealed that he wore no undershirt, sales of this particular garment slumped. By European standards, the fact that he was not wearing an undershirt betrayed the fact that he was no gentleman; but, more importantly, it served to emphasize the potency of the sexuality of the lower-class male. It was this with which cinema-goers identified.

In the end, all clothing is to do with sex, and it is sex appeal which sells styles. Edward VII, unlikely as it now seems, had it in great measure. Edward VIII did not, nor has any subsequent male member of the British Royal family.

So, in the thirties, when the fashion business and media were hyping the Prince of Wales, the real fashion icons were men like Gary Cooper and Henry Fonda, who created some of their most popular roles playing cowboys. The laid-back languor of the assured male archetypes they brought to life transferred itself to the clothes they wore: the checked shirts, suede vests, high boots and jeans which were for them almost a screen uniform. And it is the stars of the thirties and forties (the great decade of the Western movie) who, in their film roles, created the looks of the day.

The images of the cinema broke a pattern of fashion which had prevailed for centuries, giving birth to the blue-collar style leader. With rare exceptions, all previous fashion had been created by a social elite whose greatest claims were exclusivity and wealth. Now, fashion was to percolate up through the classes, instead of down.

CASUAL YOUTH

The cry 'Give us heroes' is heard in every generation. And it is always answered, with more or less success, by men as different as possible from the heroes of the immediate past. The demand for heroes in the twentieth century has largely been fulfilled by America and its media. By 1917 almost all the world's films were made in the United States. The first broadcasting station – opened in Pittsburgh in 1920 – followed close on the heels of the success of the cinema. Although television was yet to come, it is fair to say that even before the British General Strike in 1926 or the American Wall Street crash of 1929, modern culture was not only increasingly youth orientated, it was also thoroughly Americanized. Egon Larson wrote in *Spotlight on Films* (1950) of Douglas Fairbanks, 'There was no man in the audience who hesitated to identify himself with this knight of the screen, escaping from his own humdrum life into gallant adventure'. It was no more than a statement of fact. The adventures were almost always told with an American accent – and in most cases with a blue-collar one. Even the American vocabulary was snapped up by the bright and not so bright young things in Europe.

When in 1925 President Coolidge declared that 'the business of America is business,' he was behind the times. American advertising techniques, more predatory and sophisticated than those of any other nation, had already turned the people of the United States into consistent consumers. How they did so sheds an interesting light on the subject of heroes and heroines. Whereas women in popular advertisements – who were still drawn rather than photographed at this stage – were invariably refined, pretty and lady-like, men were almost always blue-collar. The Chesterfield cigarettes man ('I'll tell the world: they *satisfy*') may well wear a white shirt and well-knotted tie but these do not disguise his proletarian origins. Nor were they meant to. American men did not want their heroes to be of the stuffed-shirt variety.

In fact, stuffed shirts were beginning to disappear from both American and European male wardrobes. Dress was being deconstructed as part of the move towards egalitarianism. It was feeling the influence of the new cult of the active man, who played tennis and golf and who had also begun to be fanatical about the sun. The need to show off his newly fashionable tan made him jettison many items of dress previously considered essential. The list of rejects from his wardrobe in the 1920s and 1930s is impressive: formal dress boots, spats, gloves, canes, waistcoats and vests, stiff collars (except with a city suit), even white tie and tails; all were facing virtual extinction.

For both sexes, shedding unnecessary items of dress has been a leitmotif of the twentieth century. Some progress was made in the 1920s but how much remained to be achieved is demonstrated by a booklet published in 1930 by the London tailors Austin Reed, as a guide to what its customers should pack for their holidays. Listed under 'The Absolutely Vitals' are toiletries (including hair tonic and lavender water), stiff collars (plus spare stiffeners), links and studs – an arsenal of agony, as any man who has ever wrestled to put a back stud through a stiffly starched collar will confirm – smoking jacket, folding coat-hangers, shoe trees, shoe horn and clothes brush. For sport, special lightweight

ABOVE: Advertisement for Chesterfield cigarettes, 1920s

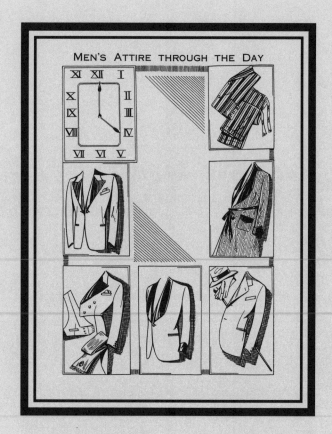

underwear was required. For evenings: wing collars, black ties, white ties, scarf, white waistcoats and patent-leather shoes. This was the Louis Vuitton cabin-trunk life, a million miles from the requirements of the modern Adidas or Puma sportsbag traveller. It is not surprising that the men who lived by such formal and proscribed sartorial rules were delighted to hit the beach at the Riviera or the Venice Lido, though it must be remembered that even in the late thirties, the Plimsoll line of decency insisted that bathing shorts did not sink below the navel and many resorts still preferred the twenties bathing suit which covered the entire torso.

ABOVE AND RIGHT: Daywear and holiday wear, from *The 'Tailor and Cutter' Year Book of Fashions*, 1934

It is hard to be formal in the sun, and even harder to be dignified. Pompous clothing was killed in Europe as much by temperature as by anything else; in the United States, it was more to do with temperament. On both sides of the Atlantic, sex was the motive and music was the medium.

The twentieth century has seen commercialized popular music become a central cultural force. It began with the jazz rhythms of the twenties and fanned out to include all age groups and cultures but its first, and perhaps most dramatic, impact was on the post-Depression young of America in the late thirties. The sordid dance marathons of the Depression, when young people danced until they dropped – for small financial rewards – gave way to something much more spirited. The late thirties and early forties saw two cultures join and intermix. The commercialism of white dance met the vitality of black. The result was bebop – a startling, sparkling reaffirmation of the joy of energetic movement to vibrant music.

On the 1940s dance floor the aim was exhibitionism and those who did it best were known as shiners. Dress was informal. The evening might well start with a tie but rarely ended as anything but open-necked. Sweaters, slip-overs, slacks and saddle shoes completed the look. Parents found everything about it irritating but its impact could not be ignored. In fact, swing gave birth to teenagers – the first autonomous youth movement in history – who came into their own in the forties on a wave of confidence brought about by increased affluence, social independence and the loosening of sexual constrictions. The casual look (part sportswear, part college-classic) derived from Hollywood but was sourced from the sportswear manufacturers based in California, whose approach – much younger and freer than that of the East Coast – was entirely independent of ideas generated by the formality of the male business suit.

American teenagers dressed in small-town style. In fact, they created the idea of informal dress as a way of distinguishing between their tribe and that of the older and more established male. It was a deliberate move, contrived and knowing, which showed a sophistication that was not apparent in teenagers outside America. In Europe, and especially in Britain, there was a certain kind of loosening up – a tie left off where one would previously have been worn, or tweeds replacing the formality of flannel – but there was no attempt to change styles and nothing as original as finding new ways of wearing existing items of clothing.

Above all, small-town American boys perfected a casual look that was so young and informal that it automatically barred entry even to those five years older, let alone to parents. Baggy trousers, loafers, work boots, dangling shirt-tails of flannel or check 'lumberjack' shirts, leather and cotton windcheaters: the ingredients of their dress codes would become, in less than twenty years, the staples of all casual dress, regardless of age.

They did not invent them. All the components were already in place. What American youth did was to relocate them, taking them from farm and forest and introducing them into suburban backyards and provincial campuses. And even if to modern eyes it looks tame and conformist, there was in fact a small touch of iconoclasm to forties dress. The dazzling white T-shirt exposed above the unbuttoned neck of a plaid shirt is a cliché today but in the forties it was a bold move to flaunt as fashion something still seen as underwear. The baggy jeans with the rolled cuffs were also sufficiently irregular and relaxed not to pass without comments about falling standards.

Such clothing was the gear for Saturdays: for tinkering with the 'tin Lizzie', listening to records or having a soda at the corner milk bar before going to a drive-in movie and ending up in the 'hot' jive-dive. From such an innocuous background the whole teenage fashion look developed. It took the world by storm in the fifties and is all-powerful today. The basis of the Preppy look, the Bon-Gout-Bon-Genre craze and the Roman Pariolini, it is now enjoying an atavistic revival in Japan.

Perhaps one reason why it was young Americans who initiated the first casual look was to do with the fact that few of them had to suffer school uniform. Within certain rules they were allowed to go to school dressed as they wished or as they could afford. So they were much more accustomed to making dress decisions – with or without parental control – than were their British counterparts. They were also the products of a school system designed to bring out their individuality rather than force them to conform to the traditions of earlier generations. All these factors made them informed and experienced dressers. But they did not make them radical, as their rejection of the zoot suit, the most exciting fashion development in the forties, makes clear.

The zoot suit was initially an African-American style which developed as part of the jazz craze and which was also adopted by young Mexican-Americans. It was the first true dandy fashion of the twentieth century in the sense that it was outsider fashion which became an almost instant thorn in the flesh of the authorities. Everything about it was exaggerated, and an affront to established taste. Long jackets, usually double-breasted and always wide-shouldered, reached to the knees; trousers were baggy in the thigh and narrowed to twelve inches at the cuff; ties were either very wide or very narrow and the hat was always a wide-brimmed fedora. Add a long watchchain and thick, crepe-soled 'brothel creepers' and you have a look which for most Americans might have come from another planet.

ABOVE: Traditional items of the middle-class wardrobe were given a new interpretation under the influence of the zoot suit. USA, 1943

The zoot suit was seen as dangerously subversive and the authorities lost no time in trying to rout it – at least from the white side of the tracks. It was declared unpatriotic, since the large amount of material it required contravened wartime rationing regulations. White servicemen took it upon themselves to discourage zoot-suit wearers by physically attacking them and stripping them of their suits. Pitched battles broke out between Marines and young Black and Mexican zoot-suiters and rioting eventually spread from Los Angeles to Detroit, Philadelphia and New York.

The obviously subversive quality of the zoot suit made it particularly popular in France, where it was adopted by a small, iconoclastic corps of young men called Zazous, who wore it in defiance of the clothing regulations established by the German occupiers. They did not want to be swamped by the grey conformity demanded by their conquerors. For the Zazous, the zoot suit was a political statement, just as it was in the ghettos of America.

Though the zoot suit came to a sorry end in postwar Britain, where it became the dress of the spiv, wide-boy and racketeer – the working-class rogue male making money as fast and as ruthlessly as the Italian working-class rogues of the Prohibition era in the United States – it lit a flame which has affected all societies. It is not surprising that the Nazis tried to stamp it out, just as, for the same reason, they tried to stamp out jazz.

Jazz, of course, was far too powerful to be killed by authority. The basis of the most liberating form of dance ever, it was kept alive in Europe by the wartime influx of the world's most exotic soldiers. The G.I.s were really no different from their counterparts in other armies, but what they had over the rest was the glamour of association. When they came to Europe, their presence seemed to symbolize the new hopes – to dress as you wished, to be who you wished, to live as you wished – which movies had brought to the world as the American dream made manifest. In oppressed countries, the fantasy of egalitarianism attached itself to the G.I.s and made them the heroes of the young. And why not? Rich and sexually uninhibited, they seemed more sophisticated than other troops. And they were generous – with gum, nylons, cigarettes and even cap badges for little boys who collected such things. Certainly their uniforms seemed smarter. But headiest of all was the fact that they spoke just like movie stars. Hollywood had made the American language the speech of the cool, casual, controlled man and it was this that made the G.I.s seem like walking aphrodisiacs in a Europe that was overawed by the American way but eager to follow it. It was inevitable that their presence would strengthen the mania for American popular culture which threatened indigenous ways of life for anyone under thirty.

In the late 1940s the American teenager's check shirt became a cult and then a craze in France while the bebopper's suede shoes were so popular with young men in Britain that it seemed unbelievable that, less than ten years earlier, suede shoes had been seen as cast-iron proof of homosexuality, so much so that the Prince of Wales had provoked something of a scandal by his fondness for them.

It looked as if youth had stormed the barricades and brought down generations of pompous dress attitudes. But the old world of fashion did not give up without a struggle. In defiance of American informality, which by the early fifties had reached the stage not only of young men walking city streets without a tie or hat, but of their actually wearing 'Hawaiian' shirts which hung loosely over their trousers, a small group of Londoners tried to recapture what they saw as Edwardian elegance.

The return to Edwardian formality was of interest only to a few men but it nevertheless managed to gain considerable publicity. That it did so was more a reflection of the kind of men involved – socially acceptable, from the better English public schools and frequently in the Brigade of Guards (where, even in the second half of the twentieth century, appearances have remained of vital importance), or employed in the media – men who both demanded attention and received it. They saw themselves as the guardians of the flame of male elegance and were already nervous that creeping casualization would eventually destroy the need for fashion change and reduce the number of essential male garments to just a handful. Lacking a coherent

philosophy, however, they failed to dominate sartorial attitudes as Brummell and his group had. But they caused a stir. Americans especially liked the formality of cut and the return to traditional standards which they saw in the neo-Edwardian look, with its long jackets with flared skirts and centre vents and its impeccably tailored trousers.

The protest of people who refused to move with the times and preferred to look backwards rather than forwards, the neo-Edwardian look was given a good press and became known worldwide. It was a class gesture strangely out of step in a country still high on the postwar cocktail of idealism, egalitarianism and a dream of one nation. In a society where, in order to survive, class had gone discreetly underground, anything as blatant and crudely propagandist as the neo-Edwardian look was bound to bring a reaction. And it did. In the mid-fifties the news came that the enemy had run off with the uniform. Mayfair affectation had been taken, vulgarized and revitalized by the East End. The working-class Teddy Boy, who had all the vigour and energy that the languid neo-Edwardian lacked, had added to the upper-class style elements of American dress, and by so doing had destroyed the very rationale behind neo-Edwardianism – the jingoistic and completely outdated assumption that British fashion for men was, almost by definition, superior to that of the rest of the world, and especially superior to anything likely to be created in America.

In actual fact, the Teddy Boy look as a working-class restyling of neo-Edwardian dress was largely a media invention. In reality, its deeply draped jackets, slim-jim ties and greasily baroque hillbilly hairstyles owed more to Hollywood than to the West End.

Like the Zazou zoot-suiters, the Teddy Boys, though well-publicized, were relatively few in number and had no effect at all either on the thousands of men in the suburbs who remained content with their standardized 'demob' suits or on the teenagers and young men happy to dress like them. Neither the neo-Edwardians nor the Teddy Boys brought anything of lasting value to fashion, apart from an attitude which, in both cases, set out to polarize. It was an early example of what was to become a recurring theme in British fashion: vitality and originality paralysed by class divisions and petty obsessions.

Once again, in postwar as in prewar fashion, the vital force came from the United States, on the back of that country's two great cultural strengths – film and pop music – and with the help of its sophisticated advertising and promotion industries. With the prescience of a culture which knows what we want before we know it ourselves, America had already scented the track that would lead to the end of the century. Everything was turning towards the idealization of youth and nonconformity, though it was not until the sixties that the middle-aged and elderly capitulated. It was American advertising and the American media which

enfranchised youth as a commercial entity, complete and powerful within itself. The uncommitted purchasing power of young Americans encouraged the media and entertainment worlds to create a culture for them alone. Predominantly based on music and rebellion, it had little appeal outside youth. Heroes became younger to suit the new order. James Dean, on and off the screen, projected a persona of moody immaturity and latent hysteria which was essentially adolescent in its self-absorption. But the real movement – the movement with all the impact lacking in the Teddy Boys – was initiated by the 1954 film *The Wild One*, starring a hero who truly looked the part: Marlon Brando.

ABOVE: Marlon Brando in *The Wild One*, 1954

The Wild One was the story of marauding gangs of leather-jacketed motorcyclists in Southern California. It was a case of art imitating life, being based on an incident that had taken place in 1947, when a town had been terrorized by drunken bikers. What *The Wild One* gave birth to was the culture of the biker, who stood for sexuality, power and nonconformity. It took informal fashion forward from being merely a cult to being a subculture which could not be ignored. What biker culture brought into the open – which appealed so much to youth and so alarmed the older generation – was the conviction that clothes could make a statement which was not about cleanliness, smartness or respect for the existing institutions, a statement which flew in the face of conformity to other's standards and which recognized prevailing dress codes for what they were – the unwanted baggage of a society based on class and paternalism. It was a movement which had to happen sometime, and which could only have happened in the United States – for all its limitations, still, in the fifties, the least hidebound country on earth. With *The Wild One*, clothes as the weapon of the underdog who sees himself as the overlord had arrived.

STYLE ON WHEELS

Over the last 150 years, sport has increasingly become the driving force behind many developments in masculine clothing. On the most popular level, cycling has had as great an influence as any other sporting activity on deformalizing the way men dress. The demands it makes today are not so different from those made on the group of young Italians photographed in Sicily at the turn of the century. Speed and efficiency – not to mention safety – require the pared-down silhouette of clothes cut close to the body and unlikely to flap around and get caught in the wheels. Today, commercial bicycles are almost as fast as racing bikes. Both travel at speeds which would have been unimaginable 100 years ago. They demand tight-fitting and aerodynamic materials such as Lycra. This clings almost as close as a second skin, offers no air resistance and provides a degree of protection in urban streets as well as open spaces.

OPPOSITE PAGE AND BACKGROUND: Vincenzo Florio (left) and his friends, Sicily, c. 1900

RIGHT: Cyclist, London, 1995

BELOW: Tour de France, 1995

DRESSING FOR DINNER

The dinner jacket – originally known as the Homburg jacket – was introduced to English society in the late nineteenth century by Lord Dupplin, who had seen it in Germany. Its informality caused much discussion, of the 'It can certainly not be worn in the Stalls, but is it permissible in the Dress Circle?' variety. Even in the 1880s such questions were important to men irked by the rigours of formal evening dress. The tuxedo, the U.S. name for the dinner jacket, had its first fashion outing in 1886, on the back of one Griswold Lorillard, who scandalized his fellow guests by wearing it to the snooty white-tie-and-tails Autumn Ball at the Tuxedo Club, in Tuxedo Park, New Jersey. Even as late as the 1920s, New York society, like that of London, still favoured the formality of tails but, by the end of the decade, the dinner jacket had found its place in the gentleman's wardrobe, thanks to the enthusiastic patronage of the Prince of Wales and Lord Louis Mountbatten. Today, it is as varied in shape, colour and texture as daywear. With young men, the black bow-tie, once the dinner jacket's essential accessory, is going the way of the white. A sophisticated cravat, loosely tied – as in the Valentino version opposite – gives the evening jacket's traditional elegance an attractive, dandified air and helps the guest to be easily distinguished from the *maître d'* and his waiters.

ABOVE: Jean-Paul Gaultier, 1997

TOP: Dolce & Gabbana, 1997

RIGHT: Catalogue of the House of Kuppenheimer, New York, 1911

OPPOSITE: Valentino, 1993

THE COWBOY

The dress of the working cowboy – especially his jeans and boots – has been so absorbed into modern urban fashion that it is now worn with confidence, and even conviction, by men who would run a mile if asked to sit in a saddle. What is it about cowboy gear that gives it such pulling power? The masculine authority that it suggests is more to do with myth than reality. There is no evidence that cowboys were more courageous than troopers or that their lives were more difficult than those of trappers, but such beliefs have sunk so deeply into our collective psyche that even the most diffident

of men can, by wearing cowboy clothes, believe themselves to be part of the hard-drinking, hard-riding, hard-fighting dreamworld into which we have turned the cowboy life. The reality was neither romantic nor colourful. Cowboy work was insecure and cowboys were among the worst-paid workers in the U.S. Because their world was climatically tough, their clothing evolved to be as impermeable as possible. Closely woven denim, cambric and tough leather had to keep out wind, rain and, above all, dust. In the end, cowboys proved to be expendable; their dress, however, seems eternal.

OPPOSITE: Cowboys, Tucson, Arizona

ABOVE: Still from *The Magnificent Seven*, 1960

LEFT: Andy Warhol, *Two Elvis's*, 1977

IN THE NAVY

Naval uniform is remarkably similar worldwide because it is based on dress codes originating in the British navy. Surprisingly, naval dress was not formalized until 1857, although a 'customary' uniform had evolved by the end of the eighteenth century, consisting of white trousers, blue jacket and tarpaulin hats. Some captains designed uniforms specifically for their crews. Even as late as 1820, the captain of the gig *The Harlequin* got away with dressing his crew as harlequins. There was already a strong tradition of sailors 'personalizing' their uniforms by adding extra buttons, hat ribbons and braid trimmings. Even after 1857 – when the uniform became a blue serge frock, trousers, a jumper with a blue collar bordered with white tape, a pea jacket, a black handkerchief and a straw hat – rules were flouted as sailors fought against uniformity. Common variations included bell-bottoms up to twice the width allowed and flannel trousers cut very low, with their tops embroidered with flowers. It is this traditional involvement with appearance which attracts Jean-Paul Gaultier to the sailor and his dress. Gaultier has made a trademark of the matelot jersey – which he himself frequently wears – using its stripes for the bottle which contains his 'Le Male' range of toiletries for men.

ABOVE: Jean-Paul Gaultier advertisement, 'Le Male', 1996

BELOW: Jean-Paul Gaultier, 1996

BELOW RIGHT: Sailors in Venice, 1970

OPPOSITE, BACKGROUND PICTURE: Captain H. Rushton, R.N. Captain of *HMS Edinburgh*, at the Diamond Jubilee Review, 1897

OPPOSITE: Gene Kelly and Frank Sinatra in *On the Town*, 1949

TEDDY BOYS

Extremes of male fashion only work on a small scale. Once they become part of the mass-produced formula their essence is lost. It is because it was taken up by so few men at the time that the Teddy-Boy outfit of the 1950s is of interest today. It was almost entirely a British phenomenon. In the United States, the decade which saw the introduction of Hugh Heffner's *Playboy* magazine was interested only in the grey worsted suit of the dependable man with a plain white nylon shirt as obligatory accompaniment. This is surprising, since the music to which the exuberant Teddy Boy danced was almost invariably from the U.S. The Teddy Boy, named after Europe's greatest royal trendsetter at the turn of the century – Edward VII – surfaced on the back of that music in the early 1950s. His dress was a pastiche of the upper-class neo-Edwardian style that had emerged from Savile Row as a patriotic gesture after the Second World War but it had many links with American Country-and-Western clothes, including the bootlace tie and heavy-soled suede shoes. It was later, in the 1960s and 1970s, that Teddy-Boy dress became more widespread as part of the rock 'n' roll music scene. By then it had added frilly nylon evening shirts in a variety of colours, faux-leopardskin brothel creepers and 'designer' touches to give an appearance of provincial theatricality which would not be recognized by the sharp East Enders who created the original Teddy-Boy look.

ABOVE: Edward VII. Portrait by XIT in *Vanity Fair, c.* 1903

RIGHT: Teddy Boy, Tottenham, London, 1954

OPPOSITE: Rock and Roll Festival, Wembley, London, 1972

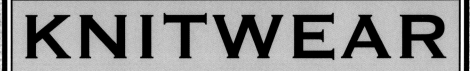

KNITWEAR

It was in the 1920s that knitwear became a recognized and legitimate item of fashionable casual dress. Found in womenswear by Chanel and Patou and in menswear on the links and in the dance hall, it was part of the new informality that emerged after the First World War. Of all the patterns of knitwear, none exemplified the between-the-wars period better than the Argyle, which was at home in socks, pullovers, knitted shirts and gloves. In the 1960s knitwear became a more complex affair of subtle patterns and myriad colours in the hands of the Italian designers Tai and Rosita Missoni, whose expensive designs were worn by the richest of the stylish and are rightly preserved by their owners as future heirlooms. Simultaneously modern and classic, they are rare in fashion in that they are completely timeless.

OPPOSITE, TOP LEFT:
James Dean in an Argyle-patterned
sweater, 1955

OPPOSITE, CENTRE LEFT:
Louis Armstrong wearing Argyle-
patterned socks, Chicago, *c.* 1930

OPPOSITE, BOTTOM LEFT:
Leslie Henson and Guy Fare, 1925

OPPOSITE BOTTOM RIGHT:
The dancers Lydia Sokolova and Leon
Woizikonovski, 1924

RIGHT: Missoni, 1983.
Drawing by Antonio Lopez

BELOW: Missoni, 1996

ITALIAN STYLE

If one name alone had to sum up the fashion miracle that gave Italy the lead in male style in the 1950s, it would have to be Brioni – the Dior of the menswear world. Bringing to ready-to-wear the skills normally associated only with bespoke tailoring, Brioni produced a luxury line of menswear which had the great advantage – still quite rare in the fifties – of merging quality with comfort. Where it led, other Italian firms followed and Italian fashion was soon at the cutting edge, where it has remained ever since. Without Brioni, it would have taken menswear much longer to reach the highpoint of Giorgio Armani in the mid-eighties.

A bastardized version of the Italian style surfaced briefly in England and travelled, even more briefly, to America, via Carnaby Street. Outside Italy, the look became less highly tailored – mainly, cynics said, because to copy real Italian style was too difficult and time-consuming, especially in the fast-moving young fashion world of London. It is true that sharp tailoring was at the time a skill that belonged to the Italians alone. Nevertheless, London Mods based their look on the silhouette and scale of the Italian masters.

MAIN PICTURE: Gregory Peck and Audrey Hepburn in *Roman Holiday*, 1953

OPPOSITE TOP: Early Brioni Roman Style label

OPPOSITE CENTRE: Sketch by Luigi Tarquini of the 'Columnar Look', launched by Brioni in 1955

OPPOSITE BOTTOM: Mod, London, 1960s

Roman Style
MADE IN ITALY

Brioni
1956

SMART STREETS

The 1950s were a watershed for the social and sexual attitudes which create fashion. They were a time when youth finally realized its power, took courage and set about imposing its own order. It was then that the first steps were taken towards ousting the Man in the Hathaway Shirt – coolly patrician and subtle in his sexuality – and moving towards the 1990s Marky Mark in his Calvins – rudely raunchy and indisputably of the people. The difference between these two classic advertising images marks the degree of change which has taken place in the past forty years.

The fifties were the last decade when one of the rites of passage from youth to maturity was the purchase of the first grown-up sports jacket. Modelled precisely on those worn by older men, the sports jacket had virtually no stylistic variations apart from colour and texture of cloth. Today, such garments are worn only by reluctant upper-class schoolboys and men in their thirties and above, but in the 1950s the sports jacket was considered to be an informal, rather relaxed, item of dress – a view based on nothing more radical than the fact that it was worn with non-matching trousers. Since it was always accompanied by a tie and often by a waistcoat, the effect was no different from that of wearing a suit, and had little to do with ease or comfort.

It was the search for comfortable dress as much as the demand for informality which

OPPOSITE: Zazou style, *c.* 1943

moved fashion forward in the fifties. The menswear industry is one of the slower moving creative areas. Traditionally, once problems have been solved, tailors have seen little point in looking out for new ones and have been content merely to reproduce variations on the same theme. Basic shapes have often remained unchanged for several generations. Even details like the width of lapels or the number of buttons barely alter from decade to decade. This stasis has always been seen within the industry as its strength, but in the fifties the young exposed it as its weakness.

The clothes-conscious young man of the fifties was not an entirely new breed. He was no longer upper class, but that could be said of many previous fashion-followers. Like his predecessors of any class, however, he knew that fashionable dress and social power were linked. As territorial as his more aristocratic counterparts, he also used his dress to define, encompass and exclude. The territory he wished to make his own was the town, not the country; the mean rather than the glittering streets of the major industrial cities. Whereas leisure had traditionally been seen as a country commodity, to be dressed in tweeds, off-duty clothes were now expected to be as cutting edge as any other aspect of city life. And the appropriate fashion look was provided by the Italians. Stiletto-pointed shoes brilliantly shining, they presented what was to be the first serious challenge in a century to the hegemony of British tailoring.

Slicing through the vaudeville exaggeration of zoot suits and brothel-creepers, Italian tailoring made a direct appeal to young men eager for an approach to dress and grooming which would cut them loose from the constraints of middle-aged fashion and provide them with an elegance unhampered by historic associations, one based on youth rather than on hierarchical principles. Italian fashion hit the rest of the world with the same force as it had in the fifteenth century. And for the same reason – sex.

Italian tailors knew how to cut clothes to flatter, but then so did Savile Row and Ivy League tailors. What made Italian style different was its point of view. Turning their backs on the accepted line, Italian tailors set out to create clothes which not only looked young but, unlike the products of traditional tailoring, only looked good on the young. They were not adapting an existing line to younger men's taste, but, much more radically, were treating young men as a completely new market. This was a fresh concept in the staid and traditional world of gentlemen's tailoring and its effect was to bring youthful fashion into the mainstream.

Carefully judged for commercial viability, these were clothes to ruffle the waters of old-guardism but not to cause a social storm. Their tailoring reflected the Italian postwar obsession with line, seen initially in its streamlined industrial design. The Italian suit, with its short jacket, high lapels and figure-hugging trousers was as modern as the new jet planes just coming

off the drawing boards. As minimalist as anything worn in the early nineteenth century, Italian fashion was also very sexy. From sleeked-back hair to thrustingly pointed toe, it turned the young male into a walking phallic symbol.

The world was moving forward fast. A new sexual and social confidence needed appropriate clothing. Apart from the zoot suits of the 1940s, fashion had changed little since the 1930s and a gap existed between the clothes available at Main Street level – traditional, classic and static in design – and the youthful turmoil just beginning to bubble up.

The narrow pants, high-buttoned boxy jackets and cut-away collars of the Italian look – the male equivalent to the mini-skirt – seemed fresh and new, even though they trailed some echoes of previous fashions. But what gave the Italian look its power was its overall completeness. It was not a pick-and-mix fashion. The winklepicker shoe was the element which really excited the fashionable young but they soon realized that it lost all its strength – not to say its point – when worn with traditional, wide-cut trousers. It demanded a sleek, slim leg, cut in the Italian style.

These were clothes for preening in and, rather to its surprise, the world realized that it was not just young Italians who wished to do that. Even the normally traditional *Esquire* began to get excited about Rome, at the time the centre of Italian menswear: 'Here are some new slacks that are turning up all over Rome,' the magazine declared. 'Very handsome in their smooth fit, narrow cut and tapered legs. The effect is a Continental version of that long-legged look that cowboy pants give . . . for all their casualness, these slacks look as suave on a bar stool . . . as they do strolling around the ruins.'

The immediate legacy of the Italian look was to make fashion a preoccupation of young men who had previously hidden behind the benign facade of middle-aged style. Fashion became – it seemed with startling suddenness – a legitimate interest for all young men. Hair styling became an obsession, cleanliness a fetish and shopping a pleasure.

Advertisers began to target the young as a powerful new commercial outlet. The first consumer magazines appeared, ready to encourage the new attitudes. In the main, they moved cautiously, balancing the new and casual against the formal and approved. The duffel coat and the velvet-collared overcoat, which in the decade immediately following the end of World War II had been the latest fashion for men, were joined by the chunky sweater – not to be worn under a jacket as sweaters traditionally were, but replacing the jacket and sometimes even the overcoat. It was a breakthrough. Although the sports jacket was already dying fast, what hastened it on its way was the new informality of the thick-knit sweater, which, along with its other advantages, did away with the need for a tie. In fact, the fastest growing style of all was the polo neck, which for many men made even the

shirt redundant. College students took to it in droves, although working-class young men, who were largely those driving fashion forward, looked for something with more fashion variety. They wanted to look sharp rather than casual, and they actually enjoyed the status which they felt a shirt and tie brought them.

Suddenly the Teddy Boys, who, for all their exaggeration, dressed more formally than casually, were no longer seen as an aberration but, rather, as the inspired stormtroopers who had established the beachhead for the new peacocks – new in attitude, in spending power and, most crucially, in age and class. In 1957, the twenty-one-year-old John Stephen opened the first of his chain of shops in London's Carnaby Street. He was answering a need as yet not entirely felt, a need that went far beyond the limits of a short thoroughfare which, ironically enough, was only two streets away from Savile Row, the home of traditional male dress, whose hegemony over fashion it would finally destroy. Intense media interest, clever publicity and a genuine desire in the young for something new, imaginative and original, ensured that within months even grandparents had heard of Carnaby Street. Garish, loud and crude, its freshness was so startling that it made menswear manufacturers feel old-fashioned and dowdy.

It is not too far-fetched to claim that although, almost without exception, the clothes on sale in Carnaby Street were tawdry and shoddily made, they had an immediacy never previously seen in traditional menswear manufacture. This was Carnaby Street's strength. Fashion – and this, for the first time *was* fashion: fast-moving, faddy and always looking for something fresh – could renew itself as soon as a trend had been declared. And it could do so cheaply. It made a whole generation of young men – in fact, the very first generation – into fashion-followers, whether they were sophisticated or simple; provincial or inner city. And, again for the first time, their newly acquired impulse to shop was catered for in precisely the same commercial way that female fashion urges were catered for. Young men had the money and wanted to spend it on the sort of clothes worn by their favourite pop stars and television disc jockeys in order to distance themselves from mainstream attitudes – attitudes not only to fashion, but also to the greater questions of life. They used their new fashion freedoms literally to clothe their new, independent status and beliefs.

Just as American youth had defined its 'loner' quality by its motorbike, European and British youth rode into battle on scooters (another Italian invention). And the gear they wore was as up to date as their wheels. Tightly cut jackets with high-buttoned collars, hipster pants, Chelsea boots – the overall impression was immaculate, but not in the manner of the Wall Street or City man. This look gave its wearer a vigour lacking in traditional tailoring, which still relied on disguising the figure with padding rather than enhancing it by cutting.

Carnaby Street was fast-paced and revolutionary where the conservative world of tailoring was slow-moving and evolutionary. The traditional tailoring world shunned dramatic change and abhorred novelty. But young menswear designers at the time – many with no experience of tailoring to inhibit them – wanted their clothes to be both new and different and were ready to follow the lead given by Carnaby Street's John Stephen.

Something was lost, however, when traditional tailoring chose to stagnate rather than to relocate itself within the exciting new youth movement. The 1960s saw fashion for men become the province of amateurs who moved too fast and jettisoned too much. The idea took hold that the young had no concept of quality and would put up with bad workmanship and the cutting of corners as long as the result was new and exciting. It is a belief which has had a malign influence on fashion ever since.

ABOVE: Opening of a 'gear' boutique for men, London 1965. At left is the pop singer Beau Brummell, accompanied by Lord John of Carnaby Street, who formally declared the boutique open

Yet good designers did exist, and these had the edge over the mass manufacturers because they worked on a small scale (often producing for only one boutique) and were therefore able to react to demand and monitor the needs of their customers with great speed and directness. Many of the most innovative young designers were known only to a select few, and worked in tiny shops and upstairs rooms in relatively out of the way places, known only to the cognoscenti.

But there were also mainstream designers working with the mass manufacturers who, having realized belatedly just how considerable the change in attitudes had been, were determined to recover lost ground. These designers, acting as a bridge between the avant-garde and the high street, exerted an immense influence. Foremost among them was Hardy Amies, a successful couturier who designed clothes for the Queen. Appointed design consultant to the high-street menswear chain Hepworth, he shook up a staid area of marketing to such an extent that all other manufacturers were forced to follow his lead. Amies understood the importance of what the Italians had brought to menswear. As he said at the time, 'Fashion today is to be classless in dress. The whole point is to be sexy.' Rupert Lycett Green would have agreed. The creator of Blades, an establishment catering to the moneyed 'man-about-town' and upper-class socialite who wanted to move away from the formality of Savile Row but was unhappy with Carnaby Street's egalitarian

approach, Lycett Green knew his market. His clothes had the assured elegance seen in the dress of the Edwardian leisured classes while at the same time reflecting the less extreme developments in Carnaby Street. A Blades suit or blazer – instantly recognized by fashion insiders – was the hallmark of sartorial nonchalance for the man who, like Lord Chesterfield, knew that clothes were important but would never dream of admitting it.

Amies and Lycett Green were trailblazers but others soon followed their lead. The most successful was John Ingram, who traded under the name John Michael. It was he who made the King's Road in Chelsea a Mecca for young men who thought themselves too sophisticated for the cheap and cheerful fun of Carnaby Street. As Carnaby Street's buying profile dropped in age to cater for the teenage market, the King's Road and John Michael set about creating their own fashionable man who was nearer thirty than twenty and more discerning than his pop-mad younger brother. John Michael clothes often seemed surprisingly formal compared with others at the time. They came under the heading of 'casual smart', a paradox that typified sixties fashion. It was a term that could also be used to describe the clothes of Tom Gilbey, the other major influence on London fashion at the time, who worked briefly with John Michael before going independent. With his own design consultancy, Gilbey wielded a considerable influence on the way men looked across a broad

men flooded every Saturday morning. The menswear equivalent of Mary Quant, he was a major force in altering fashionable attitudes.

Just how important Carnaby Street was in the history of male fashion is debatable. But as a catalyst to new thinking its effect was inestimable. Sadly, its strength has been vitiated by its use as a shorthand for the vacuity of 'Swinging London' in the sixties. In fact, the whole concept of the swinging sixties does great harm to a seminal decade, the first that could be called modern in that its protagonists largely turned their back on history and showed little interest in the future. It was indeed the first truly 'now' decade.

When did the swinging sixties start? In London, it is possible to make a strong case for the mid-fifties, when, in response to the increasingly powerful surge of popular music from America, home-grown pop stars began to appear. Often teenagers, they initiated the Peter Pan syndrome which was eventually to pull the age of social and sexual power down to levels previously undreamed of. But, before that happened, and aided and stimulated by Carnaby Street, came the pop revolution, leading to pop culture, described by George Melly in *Revolt into Style* (1970) as like a comic strip in that 'It draws no conclusions. It makes no comments. It proposes no solutions. It admits to neither past nor future, not even its own.'

British pop culture had a great deal to contend with in its attempts to conquer North

spectrum because, like Amies, his output was not limited to the King's Road or Carnaby Street – his biggest contract was as consultant to the German menswear giant, Ahler.

But it was John Stephen who was most profoundly influential. As 'King of Carnaby Street', he numbered royalty, pop and media stars among his customers. More importantly, it was to his shops that suburban and provincial young

ABOVE: Swinging sixties style was available both by mail order and from boutiques like I Was Lord Kitchener's Valet

Traditional elements of male dress space-aged by Pierre Cardin in the 1960s.
ABOVE: Cosmocorps jumpsuits from the 1969 collection
BELOW: The collarless suit - a look that was adopted by the Beatles

America, where the euphoria of middle-class life had been brought to an end in a way that was not to be experienced in England for another decade. And whereas swinging London produced an uneasy sartorial cocktail – part Italian sharpness, part working-class iconoclasm, and largely the sheer exuberance of children playing with long-denied shapes and colours – America was politically much darker. Its clothes reflected this essential soberness by being much more radical and anti-establishment than those found in Europe. Whether worn by Hell's Angels or hippies, American alternative dress was the dress of whole-hearted alienation, an alienation which made its British counterparts' love affair with pop culture and its advertising power seem nothing less than a short-changing of the new idealism.

For the next stage, Europe needed the United States to point the way. Long before 'San Francisco', Scott McKenzie's sixties' threnody to doomed youth, the drug culture had become the genuine counter-culture. In 1967, when most of the old were gazing at Armstrong and Aldrin, the eyes of the young were firmly focused on Woodstock, a cultural and social milestone that makes the Space Race seem nothing more than a megalomaniacal governmental self-indulgence of no lasting political importance or social significance.

Commercial fashion had quickly latched onto the space-age hype, in the hope that it might seduce the buying public as much as it did government technicians and scientists or television moguls excited by what it might mean for future exploitation of their medium. It did not. To most young people the space programme seemed a waste of money, time and, to use their own terminology, space. Alienated from a movement conceived in part to inspire patriotism, they found the idea of space-age fashion ludicrous. Every fashion commentator looking at menswear in the last fifty years concentrates on the space-age fashion revolution led by Cardin and his group, but in fact, though the futuristic designs they created looked exciting on the catwalk and photographed marvellously, they had no resonance for most men. In truth, there was no space-age fashion. What was called space-age looked more like a contrived fantasy from a designer's sketch-pad than a serious attempt at finding a meaningful look for modern men. The Cardin collarless jacket is perhaps the only idea which had any real appeal and this came more from its association with the Beatles than from any sense that it was a true fashion for its time.

Fashion history has not been kind to Pierre Cardin's reputation. It has denied him the enormous credit he deserves for expanding the parameters of masculine dress. He is arguably the most influential menswear designer of the twentieth century in that, like Hardy Amies, he changed attitudes to dress in men who had relatively little interest in their appearance and who would never have dreamed of walking through the doors of a boutique. He took the traditional pared-down silhouette of British tailoring and gave it a classless, timeless quality on which designers have built ever since. Cardin's strength lay in his ability to make function his chief focus. The attractive details on his clothes are pleasing for the same reason that details on a machine are pleasing – because they have a purpose. In fact, Cardin's design approach is closer to engineering than to traditional tailoring. Always interested in using new and modern materials (particularly stretch fabrics), refusing to plunder the past in order to construct the future, he is the Ove Arup of twentieth-century menswear. Indeed, it is possible that it was because he was so many years ahead of his time that his name faded and his full potential was never realized.

For young Americans in the 1960s, Parisian high-fashion designers held little interest. Even 'groovy' London was only marginally exciting. Acutely concerned by the inequalities and miscarriages of justice taking place in their own backyard, the youth of the U.S. turned their backs on American society, searching for a symbol of both their despair and their independence. They found it where others have often found it in the past – in hair. Years before the famous musical, Hippies and Hell's Angels grew their hair long not just to irritate the older generation but to protest against all those who believed short hair to be nothing less than a divine injunction. Short hair was seen as symptomatic of authoritarian, even fascist,

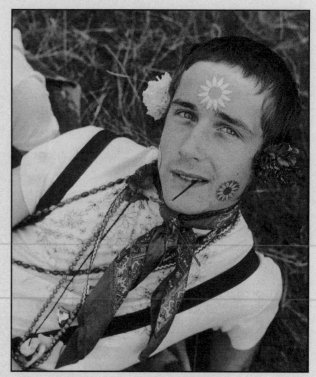

regimes. It represented the most craven caving in to old men's phobias.

Youth and age have often faced one another on the battleground of fashion. A newer conflict, one that first arose in the 1950s, is the clash between the attitudes of different ethnic groups. When Black Power began to reveal itself, and black men decided that it was culturally false to dress like whites, they went back to their roots to find an approach to dress that would be more appropriate to their new sense of political, social and sexual power. Afro hairstyles, sported by musicians such as Jimi Hendrix, were the first manifestation of this new attitude (the even more dramatic dreadlocks – a religious, rather than a fashion, statement – would come later), but it was the black approach to colour and pattern which had the most widespread effect. In fact, it is true to say that the dress of the hippies and

flower children would not have been so gloriously uninhibited had it not been for the African-Caribbean inspiration which broke down many of the sterile rules of taste besetting the white fashion world. Black attitudes to self had even more far-reaching effects. As part of the Black Power manifestation, blacks became body-conscious in an entirely new way. Long before their white counterparts, black men and women realized the value of working out and playing an active role in sport and dance. From this realization grew the most important fashion attitude of the late twentieth century – the belief that before it can be adorned, the body has to be toned, not as a matter of vanity but of health and pride. Black pride, like the gay pride still to come, was body-conscious before it became fashion-conscious. Both promulgated the belief that the only sexy body was the fit body.

American youth was the first to look beyond its own shores and cultures to embrace new attitudes en masse – to religion and morality as well as to hair-length and dress – and they returned from the hippie trails of far-flung lands much more colourful and certainly more aware than they had departed.

The broadening of the fashion spectrum for both sexes has been one of the major dress characteristics of the second half of the twentieth century. Colour, pattern and style have flooded into Western fashion from so-called less advanced cultures where more informal lifestyles mean fewer sartorial rules. They had an especially liberating effect on male fashion in the late sixties and early seventies – a time when all rules were under review, and usage was all. Russian boots, leather jackets and embroidered waistcoats; bangles, beads and headbands; skinny-rib sweaters, Indian cheesecloth shirts and shaggy Afghan sheepskin jackets not only had the advantage of being able to be worn by both sexes interchangeably, but also the ability to look remarkably authentic even when put together in ethnic mixes which defied geography.

Attitudes in the area of men's fashions changed surprisingly quickly. The father who had initially been appalled by his son's silk paisley shirt and dangling medallion began to adapt colours and textures to his own way of dressing, though most drew the line at the crushed velvet trousers in pink, purple or burgundy which became such a common sight at pop festivals. For the first time in two hundred years, colour became a major component of male fashion at all levels. But fashion's shapes – frilly shirts with extrovert jabots of lace and high, tight armholes; narrow, hip-hugging brocade coats and flared trousers – were only for the young and slim.

The ragbag of fashion mixes was important because it signalled both an end and a beginning. While it marked the end of the dominance of formal fashion aimed at the middle-aged man, it also marked the start of the fashion generation gap which is still apparent today. From this point on, young men were to have their own completely separate clothes culture.

Woodstock was a riot of crushed velvet, hand-woven fabrics, colours made from vegetable dyes – anything which signalled a total rejection of the machine-made, commercial products of U.S. big business. But there was a lot of American-pie blue jeans about the atmosphere both there and at the other pop festivals to come, which prophesied the future as accurately as Dylan's songs heralded Bruce Springsteen.

Born in the USA, blue jeans in the late 1960s still dressed the American male with a natural authority. Although even in their own country they had developed into a form of pastiche clothing – so romanticized and mythologized had the West become – they had, for Americans, a link with the heavy-duty manual worker which was to save them from future designer excesses and make them a stronger and more virile fashion in the USA than elsewhere. By wearing them, Americans were defining and identifying their own culture. For other nations, jeans, for all their popularity, were alien – their message exotic. But, either way, they were as fashion archetypally young and soon became as much part of the dress of social nonconformity as any gauzy, beaded or thong-tied item picked up on the long hauls to ancient civilizations. They were also as androgynous as most hippie dress. And, mass-produced though jeans were, the young managed to see in their blue-collar history something authentic and even organic when compared with their urban equivalent – machine-made pants in nylon derivatives, as worn by their fathers. Like a Frank Zappa lyric, they somehow seemed – to their wearers at least – to expose the sickness that lay beneath American society's obsession with getting and spending. If nothing more, they were in seriousness light years ahead of the childishly conformist Beatle jackets which exemplified the taste level of a mildly adventurous provincial draper. Already, Hell's Angels, teaming jeans with black leather jackets and heavy-duty workmen's boots, had given them a brutal masculinity far removed from the androgynous posings of David Bowie who, as Aladdin Sane, was to epitomize and articulate a powerful deviant cultural strand of the seventies.

The seventies saw colour in fashion come to glorious fruition as part of an extrovert look that had not been seen since the Incroyables. Dress and hairstyles which would have raised eyebrows even in the theatre less than fifteen years earlier were now acceptable on the most prosaic of streets. Working-class men on building sites sported hair as long as a cavalier's. Middle-class accountants grew straggly Viva Zapata bandit moustaches. Upper-class gallery owners began to affect pigtails. Jeans – which had become almost a uniform – were patched and prettified with pieces of velvet, crewel work, or lace, painted with patterns and pictures and even covered in studs, rhinestones and shards of glass. Shirt collars became so deep that the kipper tie was the only thing which could stand up to them apart from a loosely tied cravat or a length of vividly coloured silk or velvet wound round the neck. High heels and platform soles in satin glittered with diamanté – anything was acceptable as long as it was clearly anti-establishment and either socially or sexually provocative.

But other attitudes were developing as well. The seventies ended with young men being not only stridently opposed to the established order but also increasingly anti-fashion as they realized how ruthlessly the fashion system had taken over their freedoms, codified them and sold them back to their originators through the vehicle of pop music, the most commercial creative movement of the century. The time had come for new, less easily appropriated, cults.

If hippie dress was predominantly a protest by middle-class youth against a materialistic society, the new army-surplus skinhead culture developing in major cities in the Western world was something much more radical and committed. Commercial fashion was now seen as a confidence trick. To buy it was to capitulate to a society and values from which the young felt increasingly alienated. Boutiques and smart menswear shops were out; ex-army stores and workmen's suppliers were in. The T-shirt, frequently bearing slogans with a political, jokey or sexual message – a form of bonding with others of the same mind – and jeans, now ripped and shredded, often too short and pulled up high by braces, were joined by another fashion classic of the twentieth century: the Doc Marten laced working boot, soon to be known in the U.K. as the 'bovver' boot. It was part of the new macho image which had been given a cultural identity by Heavy Metal music – an image which perfectly fitted the sense of alienation felt by the young.

Hell's Angels were given an acceptable and anodyne face for middle America in the first year of the new decade with the film *Easy Rider*. Clean, idealistic and artfully inarticulate, it was a slick exercise in not frightening the horses. And perhaps it worked best as a placebo. Certainly, the sight of Peter Fonda in biker gear was pretty rather than petrifying and seemed to fit well with the other smash hit commercial success of 1970, Simon & Garfunkel's 'Bridge over Troubled Water' which was, in itself, a link between the waif-like, hopelessly romantic dream of a hippie heaven full of love, peace and flowers and the sterner realities of politics: 1970 was the year in which the National Guard shot five students of its own nation who were peacefully holding an anti-Vietnam demonstration at Kent State University. It was also the year of *M.A.S.H.*, the scatological television programme which helped Americans – and then the world – face the unbearable by laughing at it.

Vietnam's effect on clothing was huge. Army surplus gear was already popular, partly in response to the death of Che Guevara in 1967 – Guevara's face became the rallying symbol of protest on thousands of T-shirts. There are many expressions – combat chic, battlefield beaux – that can be used to belittle the anti-war dress of 1970s youth. Urban cowboys had been one thing; city storm-troopers were another. And, if it seemed strange that young men who were avoiding the draft in ever growing numbers should choose to wear the surplus clothing of an army they could support neither ideologically nor actually, it must be remembered that in a society where machismo was increasingly sold as being to do with being drafted, the young understandably wished to buy into that part of the equation, even if rejecting the rest. And those who did not – arguably the majority – wore combat gear in sympathy for those who were forced to do so by government and law.

The American serviceman assumed the talismanic stature that had once been the undisputed lot of the cowboy. The wide open spaces of the West were taken over by the jungles of the Far East as films took battle as their setting and soldiers as their heroes. The new heroes were still loners, of course, ornery and cussed men who stood out against authority and took risks just as their predecessors had. Above all, they were men's men: to be emulated by all who wanted a piece of the action, even if it were confined solely to dress.

American society was fractured by Vietnam. It took all classes and age groups a long time to come to terms with what had been done under the guise of fighting for democracy. For American men, the reluctant Nam veteran became a member of an elite. They could respond with uncomplicated relish to Robert de Niro in Michael Cimino's *The Deer Hunter* or Martin Sheen in Francis Ford Coppola's *Apocalypse Now*. And the way in which they showed their identification was in their clothing. Heavy-duty service gear – camouflage jackets, combat pants and army boots – appeared on college campuses and soon became accepted as suitable wear even for city streets. It was a classic case of subversive style becoming Main Street fashion with barely any modification. To men for whom the ethical questions of the Vietnam War meant little, it recommended itself because it was cheap and practical. (The anorak cult – one of the most important fashions for both sexes in the second half of the twentieth century – had its origins in combat gear.) Combat dress – army surplus – has remained a powerful item in the male wardrobe for the past thirty years, just as combat itself has become one of the driving forces of popular culture.

When, at the 1972 Munich Olympics, Arab terrorists killed eight Israeli competitors, it seemed to some that life was imitating art so faithfully that combat dress might be the only appropriate clothing for modern city streets. For others, there was a new sinister role model: the menacing Alec, hero of Anthony Burgess's novel *A Clockwork Orange*, played in Stanley Kubrick's 1971 film by Malcolm McDowell. This was the English version of mean city streets, with a hero who was fetishistically obsessed with his appearance and – in a deliberately oblique and deviant reference to the Savile Row smoothies James Bond and John Steed (and their impeccable dress codes) – exposed the hidden agenda in top people's dressing. It was no accident that the anti-hero wore a bowler hat, tie and waistcoat.

If in this film art lagged behind life, in that the attitudes and dress shown in *A Clockwork Orange* were already visible on the streets of London, it was nevertheless a film of considerable influence. It seemed secretly to be sanctioning what it overtly criticized: well-dressed brutality. The only difference between Burgess's hero and Bond and Steed was that Alec lacked the manners, charm and breeding which had for centuries softened the impact of upper-class ruthlessness: he was hard and callously indifferent all through. If Bond, with his arrogant sangfroid, appealed to the middle-aged and suburban, Clockwork Orange man found his fans in the urban back streets. He stood in direct line between the Teddy Boys and Spivs of the 1940s and early 1950s and the Armani-dressed terrace boys of the eighties' football stadium.

There is another strand with which *A Clockwork Orange* must be linked: the Hollywood avenging angel who achieves feats of unbelievable stamina and heroism; whether Exterminator or Rambo. Wearing shearling flying jackets, camouflage gear, and odds and ends of army surplus, including belts and boots, these are the men who influenced so many in the late seventies and early eighties. Their impact was strong not only because the look was easily and cheaply copied, but because they represented something important: the lure of the outsider, the outlaw, the man who, despite the odds, could still beat the system and, as the last reel ended, could say 'I'll be back' with total heroic authority.

The films of Mel Gibson, Arnold Schwarzenegger and Sylvester Stallone were part of the new brutalism manifest in the Doc Martens, jeans, exposed underwear, braces and pork-pie hats which became a football terrace uniform in Britain and Northern Europe in the late seventies and the first years of the eighties. It was street cred and hardness clothed in the early dress that Punk was to deconstruct for its own

ends – a code idealized and romanticized by its association with the music of the young, socially disenfranchised population of the United Kingdom. From the start, Punk music was political, and its protagonists were working class, proud of it – and dressed to show it. They were also alienated from a society increasingly in thrall to the snobbery of wealth – and they dressed to show that, too.

Punk can be seen either as the manifestation of a deeply divided culture or as a crudely

ABOVE: London Punks, late 1970s

childish reworking of old anarchies, with few, if any, of the convictions and beliefs that inspired them. What makes Punk unique is that it was the first movement to be totally inspired by music. Without the sound, there is no movement. Of course, it is true to say that rock and roll music has been the cultural basis of all youth trends since the 1950s, but what makes Punk – seen by many as rock's final dead-end fling – so much more powerful is the fact that it was created as a response to what had happened to rock and roll itself – its degeneration into self-indulgent big business.

Punk was born angry, as the names of its groups make clear. Each is a snarl, the equivalent of a sharp kick in a tender place: The Exploited, The Clash, The Damned, The Stranglers, Chaos UK. Born of disillusionment, Punk was about living in squats, surviving on benefit and being left behind by an increasingly affluent society. Punks deliberately set out to be anti-social. The Sex Pistols said it all with their banned single, *God Save the Queen*.

Not since the Incroyables in post-revolutionary France has dress been as overtly political as Punk costume. Dirty and torn, faded and frayed, daubed with anti-social and obscene commentaries, hung with Nazi regalia – it was guaranteed to puzzle, frighten and infuriate people in the cultural mainstream. As society's hostility grew, Punk became more insular. It began to be entirely self-referring, and it was this, rather than public hostility or indifference, which eventually quenched its fire. It went from being a movement which challenged society's indifference to being remarkably similar to the pop music it despised.

It was a sad end. But, in fairness, Punk was dedicated to more than pleasure. It was a movement that attempted to slant society in favour of youth, that wanted to redress the balance of opportunity and hope. It imagined, throughout its relatively short existence, that it could undermine, if not annihilate, the attitudes which underpinned capitalism. It was this simplistic thinking which destroyed what was potentially the most powerful youth movement in history.

OPPOSITE: Tartan cowboy, late 1980s

DRESSING DOWN

It has taken centuries for us to realize that, although fashionable dress can be exciting and beautiful, it is workwear that possesses true integrity and power. We now accept that functionalism creates its own beauty. This is why men are happiest in clothes which retain their link with the purpose for which they originally evolved. As this advertisement from the 1940s shows, Levi Strauss made practicality a strong selling point for their jeans and overalls. But working gear was also worn for relaxation, as the portrait of a man in Mexico City in the 1900s makes clear. Because of their simplicity and design efficiency, his clothes, though in no way conventionally fashionable, have great charm, elegance and even dignity. It is this aspect of workwear which modern designers have adapted for their runways. What could be crisper than this trio of denim-clad lads on the Versace catwalk? Although their designer-label shirts are clearly not destined for physical work, they confer a masculine credibility through their link with the blue-collar workmen of the past.

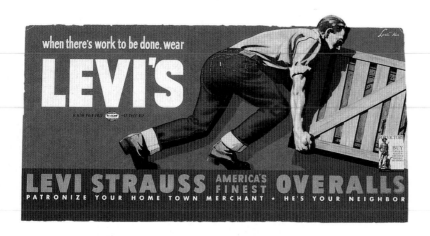

ABOVE: Levi's counter card, 1940s

RIGHT: Gianni Versace, 1993

OPPOSITE, MAIN PICTURE: Studio portrait by Romualdo Garcia, Mexico City, c. 1900

OPPOSITE TOP LEFT: Mitsuhiro Matsuda, 1993

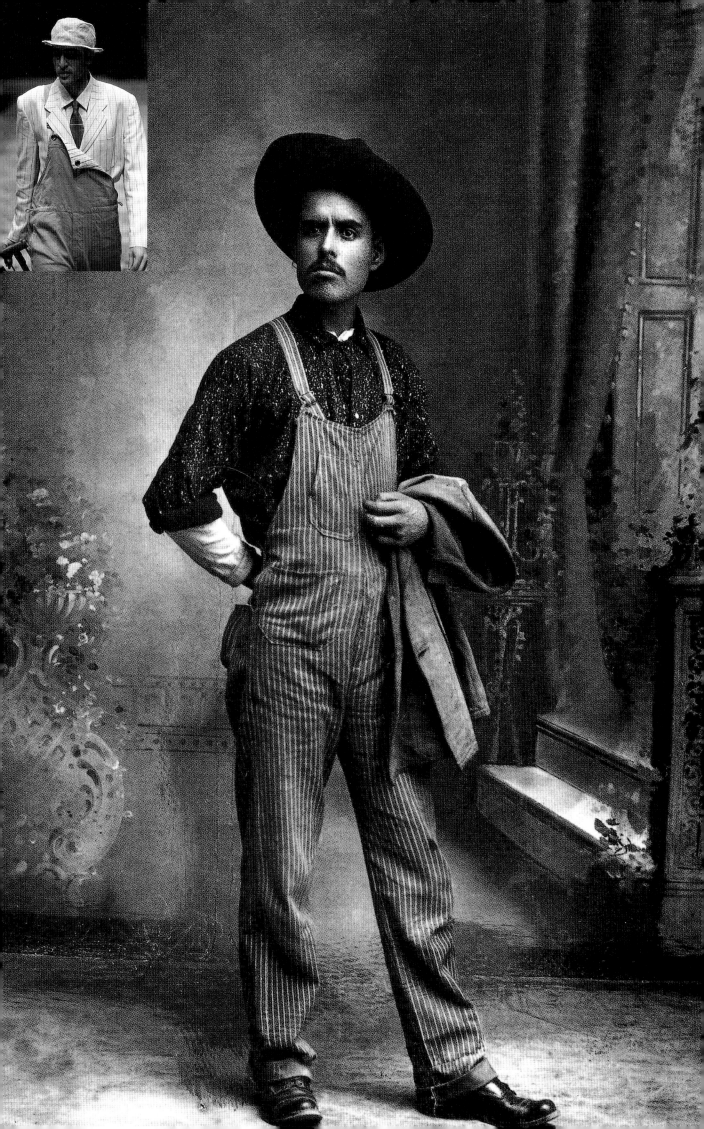

BEACHBOYS

Freedom, colour and sexuality are the basics of swimwear – and they are not always achieved by stripping down to brief costumes. Nineteenth-century beach dress, knitted, cumbersome and awkward in the water, was resented by men who, until Victorian puritanism took hold, had bathed in the nude. By the 1920s, the sleeveless, deep cut, all-in-one bathing suit – shaped like a singlet ending in pants – was considered both proper and chic. When decorated with abstract fish, as in a 1914 design by the Italian futurist painter Giacomo Balla (left), the effect was remarkably similar to modern cycling gear. But things were moving fast. The notorious American Park Superintendents' 1917 ruling that swimsuits could not expose the chest below a line level with the armpits was swept aside in the 1930s by the invention of Lastex, which made topless suits for men common. Jockey bathing trunks appeared in 1935, and for the next forty years brevity was all, though there have recently been isolated and usually unsuccessful attempts to revive the all-in-one.

MAIN PICTURE: Walter Sickert,
Bathers at Dieppe, 1902

OPPOSITE TOP: Giacomo Balla
design for a swimsuit, 1914

OPPOSITE BOTTOM: Swimsuits by
Ally Capellino and by Gazelle, 1990

LEFT: Versace, 1993

HOODLUM HEROES

Quite how a fashion goes downmarket is extremely difficult to track. In the 1920s, as the striped suit went upmarket to become the dress of the boss class which had finally forsaken the formality of the frock coat as businesswear, a counter-movement was taking place. The same staid, respectable striped suit – symbol of reliability and conformity – was enjoying an altogether more louche new life on the streets of New York, Detroit and Chicago as the dress of the dude gangster, the hoodlum immortalized in Hollywood films. Here was a man who was not only decidedly not a gentleman but had no interest in becoming one. Although the cut and quality of the gangster suit were not so different from those of the traditional suit, subtle changes were made which undermined the suit's old authority and gave it a new one. Whereas no gentleman would wear a dark shirt and light tie with a suit, the gangster did – just as he wore a soft-collared shirt when gentlemanly code demanded a stiff collar. And even though the gangster suit was almost always double-breasted, it lacked the formality of its mainstream counterpart. The gangster did not care. In fact, he dressed deliberately to subvert the standards of an establishment with which he was at war. Nowadays, tastes and styles are not so rigidly enforced. Even thirty years ago, the Thierry Mugler clothes shown below would have been rejected by anyone wishing to be a gentleman, but his modern counterpart would be attracted by their cool.

MAIN PICTURE: Still from the film *Public Enemy*, 1931

FAR RIGHT: Dolce & Gabbana, 1996

LEFT: Thierry Mugler, 1992

POWER
PADDING

The 1987 film *Wall Street*, starring Michael Douglas, looked at the manipulation of money by people who dressed in a modern version of the clothing chosen by the nineteenth-century merchant classes. Powerful shoulders, important lapels and loosely gathered trousers were the essence of the look, which suggested a physically fit, sporty body beneath clothes that have been described as ideal for making money in. Whereas many find the look disagreeable – smacking as it does in the film of pushy, preppy predators – few would deny its strength and even sexuality when presented with the confidence and elan of Hugo Boss. When the well-cut jacket is removed as a sign that serious business is about to begin, the athletic body is highlighted and constrained by flamboyant braces – surely a late-twentieth-century equivalent to the codpiece. The other element of power dressing is the expensive watch, which conveys much the same message – and with the same lack of subtlety – as the golden jewelry of the Nawah of Junagad, photographed in his magnificence more than one hundred years ago. But it is the power brokers of the Renaissance who most understand how to use dress to intimidate the opposition, which explains the prodigious width of Francis I's shoulders.

BOSS
HUGO BOSS

MAIN PICTURE: Still from the film
Wall Street, starring Michael Douglas,
1987

RIGHT: Jean Clouet, *Francis I*, *c*. 1520

BELOW RIGHT: Nawah of Junagad,
c. 1890

OPPOSITE BOTTOM: Hugo Boss,
1996

CONTRASTS

Throughout history, the male leg has been more often exposed than concealed – and as much a symbol of power as a provocation to desire. It was only in the nineteenth century that its shape was permanently covered up by the introduction of trousers, initially considered so outrageous by the old guard that the writer and clothes expert Edward Bulwer-Lytton blamed them for a breakdown of social standards. He wrote with evident disapproval in 1825 that 'fast talk and slang came in with trousers'. By the 1920s, however, they were part of establishment dressing and any attempt radically to modify their shape was strongly resisted. The 'Oxford Bags', which were introduced by undergraduates at Oxford University, were so extreme that they became a craze among young men on both sides of the Atlantic, to the great disapproval of their elders. First introduced in the U.S. by John Wannamaker of New York in 1925, their 22-inch bottoms appealed to young college boys, who took to them immediately, confident that this was a fashion that could only possibly be followed by the young. In the 1980s, exactly the same attitudes prevailed when trousers became so narrow and figure-conscious that they began to resemble a second skin.

ABOVE LEFT: The fashionable man, London, 1922

OPPOSITE: Street fashion, London, 1987

Young men in casual clothes based on sportswear are icons of the late twentieth century, their power equivalent to that of gladiators, *condottieri* and musketeers in the past. Rakish, overtly masculine and totally relaxed in their sexual confidence, they take their dress codes and attitudes to self from the narcissistic world of commercial sport. Whether their clothes are designed in Italy or Japan, they are invariably based on American college and sporting dress. The effect is powerful and so overtly 'Jock' that it has raised cotton jersey (used ubiquitously for 'sweats') to a cult level. It is easy to see why its associations with hard physical work, competition and pain give the perfect profile for millions of men whose minds are fixated on working out at the gymnasium.

IN THE
LOCKER ROOM

ABOVE:
Moschino, 1997–98

RIGHT: André
Breton, 1930.
Photo by Man Ray

FAR RIGHT:
Gianni Versace,
1984–85

BELOW: Bertolt
Brecht, 1928

LEATHER

Marlon Brando in his Perfecto jacket set the tone which black leather has retained ever since. It says clearly and curtly: bad boy. He was followed by James Dean, Gene Vincent and Elvis Presley, who gave it the added cachet of the dress of legends. But it is its uncompromisingly anti-social history which has made leather attractive to those who prefer to stand outside the norm: the critics, thinkers and creators who are seen by many as the intellectual bad boys of the century.

Whereas society accepts animal skin in a suede version, leather has always made it nervous. Not only does it have sexual overtones which many find disturbing, but it also carries with it memories of totalitarian brutality of the kind suffered by Europe between the wars. Secret police and private armies have worn leather in order to give the appearance of a carapace of strength which cannot be breached. This in itself lends an impression of sexual power which is transferred to today's wearer of leather. The illusions of strength and inviolability are, however, confined to black. Brown leather has no such connotations.

ABOVE: Punk, London, 1986

BELOW:
Marlon Brando in
The Wild One, 1954

SEXING IDENTITY

Modern attitudes to masculine identity, sexuality and dress were formed in the 1970s. They came to fruition on the pages of magazines such as *Arena* in Britain and *GQ* in America. Suddenly, or so it seemed, sexy men, fresh from their work-out in a California gym, were gazing unblinkingly at the camera, in the Rockies, in the Nevada desert, or by a Palm Springs poolside – any location where they could either wear very little or else be bundled up into butch layers of expensive clothes, like trappers who shopped exclusively at Brooks Brothers and Bloomingdale's.

On the other side of the camera, as often as not, was Bruce Weber, the photographer who took the Arrow shirt man, the 1920s college kid in his raccoon coat and the motor mechanic and farmsteader of the 1930s, rolled them all together in a rich layer of idealism and sentimentality and produced the new man of fashion: young, muscular and sporty. Weber made him look as appealing as a newborn bull calf – and roughly of the same level of intelligence.

Gorgeous but dumb, he was an instant new icon, encouraging young men to pump iron, push pills and generally make a fetish of themselves as objects of beauty. Nothing so overtly narcissistic had been sanctioned since Cassius Clay (later Muhammad Ali) remarked that he was pretty, a comment which broke the mould of how men were expected to see each other and how whites were supposed to look at blacks. Laughed at when it was made, it was a

comment which nevertheless helped change attitudes, even if only in a minor way. As a red-blooded boxing hero, Clay could make people accept what would have alarmed them if spoken by an interior decorator. And, for a time at least, his self-assessment could not be contradicted: he was, after all, the greatest in physique as well as in boxing skills.

But if Clay was mocking the shibboleths of society while appearing to be both artless and unsophisticated, Bruce Weber's approach to male beauty – and its essential corollary, sex – was totally serious. And the society in which he was articulating his point of view was different. What had made it so was gay culture, which had become a force to be reckoned with not only socially, culturally and politically but also commercially. The rise of pink purchasing power did more to change traditional attitudes to gays than all the marches and pride put together. It altered the very concept of what a homosexual man might be. Out went the traditional

European pansy, lightly rouged, voice extravagantly cadenced, mincing and simpering in a pastiche of the trivial side of femininity. In came the American model, glad to be gay, butch as the next man, determined to display his credentials as a man among men.

He was an instant hit. The relaxed approach to sexual mores which increasingly characterized some U.S. states in the seventies meant that many large towns had their gay clubs, restaurants, gyms and, above all, bath houses, where the activity was intense and uninhibitedly physical – so much so that it was joked that a gay bath house was more butch than the locker room of the Boston Red Sox or the assault course at Key West. The new-style pride in masculinity found a quick echo in dress. No more longing for the softly refined; no more chiffon or silk scarves glamorously tied around ageing necks; no more jewelry for boys. Instead, the rough check shirt and levi's, the sneakers and jogging shoes, the sculpted vest, the satin gym shorts, the jungle

ABOVE: The man of action becomes a fashion icon. Drawing by Antonio Lopez, 1970

fatigues, the work boots, the Long John
undershirt – just like heterosexual men.

But not quite. It is not just by clothes
themselves but also by the way they are worn
that attitudes are articulated. In fact, gay men,
with their heavy black moustaches, earstuds
and leather regalia, frequently looked even
more butch than their straight counterparts.
The message was as challenging as it was
unequivocal. It marked a new openness in
the gay community and demanded the same
openness in the rest of society.

And, by and large, straight men toed the line
marked out for them by gays. So much so, that
their dress actually copied gay butch style,
though not for long. The age-old homosexual
habit of turning into faggots when two or three
are gathered together soon made the leather-
work-fatigues scene seem as suspect as the limp
wrist. And the heavy moustache became – and
remains – the hallmark of the predatory
homosexual in many societies.

But the mould had been broken. Gay
men realized that effeminacy was no longer
a prerequisite of their state. In fact, muscular
sexuality – at least in appearance – was what was
required for success in bar or bath-house.
Knowing that they had a lot of fun to catch up
on and sensing, perhaps, that the newfound
liberties could not be relied on to last for ever,
gays were in a hurry to get what they could
before the pendulum of society swung against
them once more.

Gay semiotics – the shorthand of dress – was
born: to the outsider, arcane and mysterious; to
the gay man, an essential semaphore system.
Items of dress used to signify proclivities and
needs soon became standard in the young gay
scene in California, New York and most major
U.S. cities in between. For signalling purposes
the body was split down the middle as decisively
as it had been by medieval parti-coloured dress.
Adornment of the left side meant that the man
was sexually aggressive; items worn on the right
signified sexual passivity. A blue handkerchief in
the hip pocket was to be read quite differently
from a red one – and both messages changed if
pockets were reversed. House or car keys became
signifiers of homosexual activity when worn
prominently displayed. Like earrings, their
message varied according to whether or not they
were worn on the left or the right. To the
heterosexual, it all seemed unnecessarily complex.
Eventually, gay men agreed and the codes
disappeared. What remained, however, was the
confidence which the freedom to proclaim one's
sexuality had brought, and it is against the
background of America's pre-AIDS gay scene that
the 1980s attitudes to male dress must be read.

Homosexuality was not only liberated in the
seventies, it was also romanticized as being an
essential part of the wilderness tradition which
was to lead directly to Ralph Lauren, a designer
who knew a great deal about glamorizing the past
and, especially, about making the dream of the
West a valid form of dress for urban streets and

social conformity. The ground he worked had already been commandeered by the homosexual romanticizers, who saw their behaviour and attitudes as being part of a direct line of American literary and artistic tradition. Thoreau's *Walden*, Whitman's *Leaves of Grass* and Mark Twain's *Huckleberry Finn* joined Thomas Eakins's painting *The Swimming Hole* as seminal works in the gay march towards sexual acceptance – and were used by many to give a tradition and justification to that acceptance.

Inevitably, hanging over everything like a benign miasma was the myth of the cowboy, the ultimate identification symbol for the new homosexuality. The cowboy's machismo was enhanced by social historians, who pointed out that, with 35,000 cowboys riding the range in the mid-nineteenth century, often remote from townships and largely bereft of female company, it would be unlikely if some – even a majority – were not finding some sort of sexual release with one another: precisely the assumption on which Andy Warhol's 1968 film *Lonesome Cowboys* was predicated.

If gays twisted the Western myth a little to fit their philosophies, they were not alone. The backwoodsman was a mythical figure for all Americans, made specific by gay culture in the form of lumberjack dress: jeans, heavy plaid shirt and solid working boots. Menswear designers also recognized his commercial potential.

To talk of menswear designers pinpoints a vital shift in itself. For most of the twentieth

century male dress was in the hands of tailors. Even in the swinging sixties, most of the men who designed the 'way-out gear' which helped to define the youth and pop movements of the time were tailors in the unfashionable parts of London and New York. An exception was The Beatles' suit, which, with its collarless, boxy jacket and hip-hugging pants, was the first convincing mass-market example of unisex fashion. It was inspired by the suits made for Pierre Cardin (before he entered menswear) by Gilbert Feruch, pillar of French tailoring. But it was created by Cardin himself, working very much as a fashion designer rather than as a tailor.

The line between the two was blurred even in the sixties. Was Hardy Amies, dressmaker to the Queen, employed by mass-middle-market manufacturer Hepworth as a tailor or a designer? How would Tommy Nutter, Savile Row's *enfant terrible*, have described himself? A ceaseless innovator, unconstrained by the dictates of traditional taste, Nutter learned his trade in Savile Row and was dedicated to the highest standards of tailoring and yet he brought a designer's sensibility to his work. His belief was that a man of fashion should change his image and renew his style as frequently as a fashionable woman.

The tailor/designer dilemma was common to all the menswear centres of the world. In the sixties in Paris, Jacques Esterel, who once called himself a 'self-made man in the world of high fashion', concentrated on the unisex look, using jersey to avoid a confrontation with traditional tailoring skills evolved by working with mainstream fabrics. Angelo Litrico staged some of the first menswear fashion shows in Italy when he presented his men's collections in Rome in the fifties. His clothes were bought by John F. Kennedy, President Nasser of Egypt and Nikita Khrushchev. Although they had a high-fashion content, Litrico always considered himself to be a tailor.

In a sense, the issue was shelved in the seventies when fabric, colour and pattern became more important areas than cut in commercial menswear but, even then, Ralph Lauren was

designing, not tailoring, clothes. His approach was mass-market, though high-quality. The rigour of tailoring was never the major concern. As was to be expected from a man who started his fashion career working at Brooks Brothers, Lauren took a classic approach, though his Beau Brummell company which revitalized the design of U.S. neckwear and made the kipper tie a high-fashion item was, for its time, bold, if not revolutionary. But it was classic nostalgia that made Lauren's name. Brought up in the Bronx, he knew the difference between being cool, even flash, and going over the top into the over-decorated, over-designed and overstated clothing so often produced by menswear designers, many of whom are unable to resist the influence of the female fashion style of the moment and end up creating an effeminate pastiche which is of limited appeal to anyone, gay or straight. Lauren's impeccable and sexually unambivalent eye has helped him avoid these pitfalls.

But by the early 1980s the high ground of profile had been snatched from him by his fellow Bronx-bred designer, Calvin Klein. The first to use male sex to sell clothes, Klein hit the mood of the moment so squarely that it is not inconceivable that future social historians writing about America (and, indeed, further afield) will refer to the first few years of the eighties as the CK era. Certainly, in terms of sales and publicity, those years were indisputably prime Klein time.

Klein's achievement was to take the male body out of the gay closet and give it a much

ABOVE: Off-the-peg clothing made acceptable. An advertisement for Tommy Nutter's Ready to Wear Collection, 1980

wider application than the jock locker room. He did this through underwear, formerly the most unerotic item in the male wardrobe. Klein brought to underwear a gloriously flamboyant new life and changed attitudes by doing so. His vision was made reality by Weber, who photographed men in underwear for the original publicity campaign. Weber's images were disturbingly intimate exercises in homoeroticism. Their power lay not in their overt sexuality but in the narcissistic self-love of the models. These were men, the message said, who required neither women nor their own sex for gratification. Their perfectly beautiful bodies and their Klein underpants were all they needed. By making the men self-absorbed and remote, the pictures followed the classic advertising rule of presenting a challenge. It was almost as if Weber's photographs were saying to men, 'Try it, and see if CK underwear makes *you* feel as good,' while defying women to take on the task of breaking through the erotic carapace of masculine self-love.

New York – and, indeed, the world – was given the message at full throttle when Klein's enormous billboard was erected in Times Square in 1982. It showed a perfectly formed male in Klein underpants who leant back, eyes closed in semi-ecstasy at his own sensuality, released by what he was wearing. The image was so specifically sexual that it not only made CK underwear an essential for every man under thirty, but also spawned another 'first': women

began buying the underwear for themselves. Fashion magazines featured women wearing Klein underpants and a new craze was born.

What also made Klein underpants an unavoidable item for both sexes was the fact that they had the designer's name boldly printed around the waistband. Here, Klein had quickly picked up on a young male craze for wearing jeans slung so low that the top of the underpants was exposed. As the fad developed, the Calvin Klein waistband became the only one fashionable young men wanted to show off. Soon the desire for Calvin Klein underpants seemed universal. Like all fashion crazes it moved rapidly from being shockingly new and original to being ubiquitously banal, but, although an international bestseller, it was saved from becoming boringly predictable by the power of its annual advertising campaigns, through which Klein updated and renewed the visual – and sensual – excitement.

His most inspired move was to commission fashion photographer Steven Meisel to photograph the rap star Marky Mark in Calvin Klein jeans and underwear, naked from the waist up. The images were an immediate *succès de scandale*. Marky Mark's jeans were pulled down provocatively low, their fabric artfully arranged so as to conceal while seeming to reveal. Fashion had not only become totally body-conscious, but now also openly homoerotic. Yet the Meisel images struck a chord with men (and their girlfriends) who were in no sense gay. Klein had

brought the watershed age of sexual credibility down from the mid- to late twenties, where it had hovered for some decades, to well below twenty-five and even twenty – an age when bodily perfection could be both attained and retained. There was also a subtle change of image. When the sexual ideal had been an older man, dark hair had been preferred – in the 1940s and 1950s the blond man had been seen as lacking in virility. Then, Clark Gable and Errol Flynn were the types to be emulated – blonds like Leslie Howard were considered more ethereal and less earthy in appetite. But with hippies and flower power the popular sexual type changed. When sex and youth were made almost synonymous by the media, the young blond boy, seen in Visconti's 1971 film of Thomas Mann's *Death in Venice*, became the new ideal. Weber added muscles and the new archetype of sexuality was created, leaving smouldering dark looks of Mediterranean and Latin-American origin as a sub-genre.

pulled off the marketing coup of the eighties by taking items of working-class dress fetishized for generations by the gay community in their fantasies of male virility and adding to them his own contribution. Jeans and white sweatshirts were now joined by underpants as erogenous high fashion – all, of course, prominently labelled.

Klein's advertisements marked another important trend. The bodies chosen for his advertisements were young. They were also unnaturally well-developed, with the torsos of the body-builder and work-out freak, and the muscles of the dedicated sportsman. They

As the Californian beach boy and the Australian surfer became the romantic ideal, shoulder-length hair bleached by sea-salt and sun made the new Baywatch sex symbol seem like the brother to Botticelli's Primavera. Men had not only entered the era of sports and fitness, but the young man had become the sexual model for the times and the young man as athlete became a potent symbol, one which marked a new mood in male iconography and also created a new sexual type: the toy boy.

ABOVE: The label says it all. Calvin Klein Underwear, 1996

It was not until after World War I that sport became an occupation – or even a preoccupation – of men other than the gentry and upper classes. Quite simply, sport as a pastime or hobby – which is all it was in those days before it graduated to a world obsession – requires leisure. Working-class men had very little free time. By the 1950s, however, sport had become a panacea for the working man, though he was as likely to watch professional games as to play sport himself. In the crucial fight for self-expression which characterizes the late twentieth century, the sportsman has become the modern gladiator, his appearance slavishly copied by the ordinary man in the street. The professional sportsman – well-known, highly paid and over-publicized – has become the beau ideal, complete with expensive haircut and immaculate suit.

What originally captured the imagination was what might be called the 'workwear' of sport. Previously unglamorous and utilitarian items of dress such as sweats, running shorts and training shoes became invested in the 1980s with an almost talismanic glory reflected from the gladiatorial status of international sports stars. Advertisers, realizing that there was a potential pot of gold at the end of this particular little rainbow of hero-worship, used these stars to advertise training gear for wear by the general public. It worked amazingly well. Sportsmen joined pop stars as the new gods – gods whose names could sell anything associated with their world, even previously unglamorous fizzy drinks for invalids. The sweating, muscular jock relaxing after a tough work-out, drinking from a can whose liquid spilt suggestively down his body, became a cliché of eighties advertising.

Not so great a cliché, however, as the baseball cap – the archetypal sports item transferred from stadium to street. Originally a practical piece of headgear which protected the eyes of players from the glare of the sun, the baseball cap became one of the fetishes of late-twentieth-century dress, its sports credentials conferring status and sexuality on the wearer. And it was not alone. Even though the intense eighties, when the brand of trainers a young man wore was a crucial issue, have passed, dress linked to the glamour of sportsmen still has considerable consumer power. Lycra cycling and athletic shorts, vests and sweats are marketed not on the different merits of each brand but solely on the names of the heroes of the track and sports field who endorse them. Such sportsmen are the modern musketeers, the commercial mercenaries who are gladly followed into the minefield of fads, crazes and obsessions created by their appearance. *Continued on page 193*

FUNKY

The 1970s were a period of self-confidence, when many young men had the courage to step out of line and create their own fashion statement in a world where conformity was still the norm.

Those who find that courage are usually rewarded and young men have never dressed so freely as they did in that decade. What conventionally suited man could hope to rival dancer Lester Wilson's relaxed informality? His bracelets, diamond rings and fur coat may traditionally belong to the female wardrobe, but he confers on them a totally masculine charm.

When men decide to push back the boundaries, they need know no limits. Snakeskin boots with high heels, gold lamé trousers, seventies flares as wide as any Oxford bags and sealskin coats are only some of the joys awaiting those with the spirit to follow the beat and get funky.

OPPOSITE: The dancer Lester Wilson, 1970

TOP: The Italian architect and designer Ettore Sotsass, *c.* 1970

ABOVE: Northern Soul, Leeds, 1975

RIGHT: 'Rare Groove', 1988

BLACK

Black is the colour of authority, intellectuality and probity. It is also the most flattering of all colours. No men ever looked more urbanely elegant than those who, like the Brown brothers painted by Isaac Oliver in 1598 or the stern man of power delineated by Nicholas Hilliard a few years earlier, chose black in order to impress the world with their appearance. Black is unusual in having attained its status originally through the Church, a standing which was strengthened by its acceptance in courts across Europe, from Burgundy in the fifteenth century to Spain in the sixteenth. It finally achieved a universality with the merchant classes of seventeenth-century Holland, from whom it had spread to all Western societies by the nineteenth century. By then, its religious asceticism had been considerably watered down and it had achieved a certain literary romanticism.

Black also carries associations of power and of evil, and this is what gives it its sexual allure. The black-clad figure is at once terrifying and seductive, whether a Spanish courtier of the time of Philip II, a Hell's Angel, a Punk or a Goth. Even the plain black suit of a banker or civil servant contains a hint of menace. Fashion has its own way of playing with black in its games of love and death.

OPPOSITE TOP: Nicholas Hilliard, miniature portrait, 1572

OPPOSITE FAR LEFT: Yevgeny Yevtushenko in Egypt, 1970s

OPPOSITE LEFT: Alexander McQueen modelling Comme des Garçons, 1997

TOP RIGHT: Drawing by Sem, c. 1900

CENTRE RIGHT: Isaac Oliver, *The Brown Brothers*, 1598

RIGHT: El Greco (1541–1614), *Man with His Hand on His Breast*

ARMANI

Few designers have explored the purpose of dress in the twentieth century with the brilliance of Giorgio Armani. His radical – even revolutionary – approach to male dress never fails to question the function of clothes in the artistic and cultural life of our times. Beginning in the 1970s, he has honed his ideas to such a degree of sophistication that he has created an archetype which will surely continue into the next century. Gentle as a whisper, his clothes have shown us what male dressing should be. Body aware but not constraining, body-enhancing but never brash, his way of thinking is now seen as the norm in male dress. The Armani look can be worn by all age groups with confidence because, like Chanel's fashion for women, it eschews gimmicks, ignores fashion fads and springs from a philosophy based on an understanding of men's needs and a faultless technique which brings its own logic to everything the designer creates. Giorgio Armani is the undisputed genius of male fashion in the second half of the twentieth century.

LEFT: Giorgio Armani, 1996. Photo by Peter Lindbergh

RIGHT: Giorgio Armani, Evening Wear, 1989

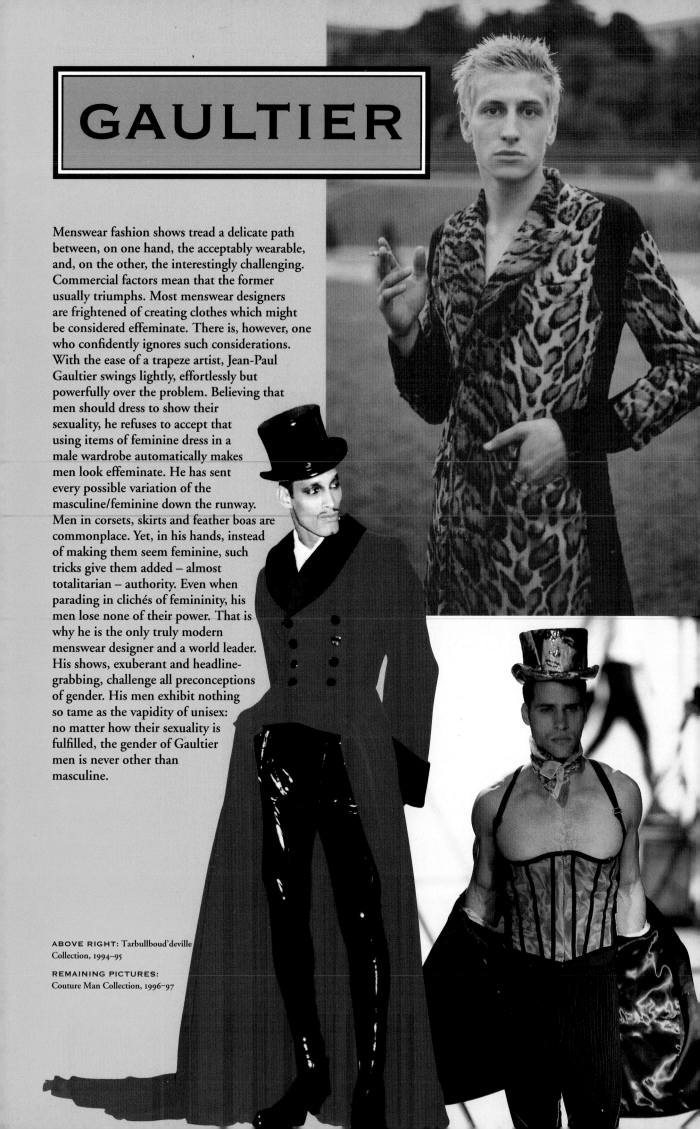

GAULTIER

Menswear fashion shows tread a delicate path between, on one hand, the acceptably wearable, and, on the other, the interestingly challenging. Commercial factors mean that the former usually triumphs. Most menswear designers are frightened of creating clothes which might be considered effeminate. There is, however, one who confidently ignores such considerations. With the ease of a trapeze artist, Jean-Paul Gaultier swings lightly, effortlessly but powerfully over the problem. Believing that men should dress to show their sexuality, he refuses to accept that using items of feminine dress in a male wardrobe automatically makes men look effeminate. He has sent every possible variation of the masculine/feminine down the runway. Men in corsets, skirts and feather boas are commonplace. Yet, in his hands, instead of making them seem feminine, such tricks give them added – almost totalitarian – authority. Even when parading in clichés of femininity, his men lose none of their power. That is why he is the only truly modern menswear designer and a world leader. His shows, exuberant and headline-grabbing, challenge all preconceptions of gender. His men exhibit nothing so tame as the vapidity of unisex: no matter how their sexuality is fulfilled, the gender of Gaultier men is never other than masculine.

ABOVE RIGHT: Tarbullboud'deville
Collection, 1994–95

REMAINING PICTURES:
Couture Man Collection, 1996–97

STRIPES

The striped suit is an essentially urban fashion statement. Its wear in the country is confined to clergy, medical men and lawyers. For that reason, even today it is the dress of authority. Invariably set against a dark background – grey, black, navy or, very occasionally, brown – there are two basic stripes: chalk and pin, both of which, fanciful folk have suggested, symbolize the ruled ledgers found in the nineteenth-century counting houses where striped suits were originally worn. In fact, in the past 100 years, striped suits have risen in social esteem. Originally the dress of lower-middle-class clerks not sufficiently exalted to wear the striped trousers and plain black cut-away frock coats of their masters, they have become universal with the demise of morning dress. Today they also have a following among the fashionable young which suggests that their future is secure. The elegant drawing from the New York House of Kuppenheimer (below), showing two highly stylish young men of 1911, and the immaculately tailored John E. Jackson (opposite), photographed in 1928, would hardly feel out of place with the young man in the modern suit by John Richmond, though his choice of neckwear with a formal suit would certainly puzzle them. And this is the secret of the universality of the striped suit. Its fabric gave it a perfection very early on and even the most inventive of subsequent tailoring efforts have failed permanently to affect its basic shape and – perhaps more importantly – its aura of respectability.

JOHN
RICHMOND

OPPOSITE TOP: Advertisement
for John Richmond, 1996

LEFT: Chalkstripe

FAR LEFT: Catalogue of
the House of Kuppenheimer,
New York, 1911

ABOVE RIGHT:
John E. Jackson. Photo by Richard
Samuel Roberts, 1928

RIGHT: Pinstripe

DECADENCE

Decadence is such a bedrock of humanity that it is present in all ages. But, for the majority of the twentieth century, it has largely been hidden from view and available only in the seaports of Southern France, the louche backstreets of certain German cities and the gay club scene of America in the late 1970s and 1980s. The 1990s saw a welcome and very public reinvention of decadence by the world's most famous designers, who have delighted in confusing gender, making the male sex more outrageously decorative than the female and exposing fetishistic clothing to an audience often previously totally unaware of it. They show the limitations of their vision by parading men not in the normal trappings of femininity but in the crude and vulgar dress of the whore. Furs, feathers, sequins and corsets are expected to provide an extra frisson of shock when worn by muscular archetypes of masculinity. How many men will ever be seduced by this circus-ring approach to dressing is, however, doubtful.

ABOVE: Dolce & Gabbana, 1995–96

TOP: W & LT (Wild and Lethal Trash), 1995

LEFT: Vivienne Westwood, 1996

OPPOSITE: Vivienne Westwood, 1997

BODY
BEAUTIFUL

Beginning in the late 1970s and gaining momentum in the 1980s, the emergence of the semi-naked male as a fashion icon has brought about a mini-revolution in advertising. In his 1981 fashion illustration *opposite*, Antonio Lopez combined the idealized forms of classical sculpture with the disturbing imagery of surrealism. By the mid-1980s, in both fashion shows and advertisements, it was the boys who were stripping off while the girls remained demurely clothed. But the new male body was not a thing of grotesquely knotted muscles or upper arms the thickness of a normal man's waist, in the Mr Atlas tradition. Masculinity was – and still is – about young, toned bodies, tightened by exercise and diet but not distorted by pumping iron. These are not unreal heroes from some fantasy of Superman but identifiable objects of desire.

ABOVE: Vivienne Westwood, 1996

BELOW: Arnold Schwarzenegger
in *Pumping Iron*, 1976

RIGHT: Advertising campaign for Valentino underwear, Autumn/Winter 1996–97. Photo by Satoshi Saikusa

OPPOSITE: Illustration by Antonio Lopez, 1981

'PUMPING IRON'
Arnold Schwarzenegger

In the Vietnam and post-Vietnam era the soldier was the hero of young men who had been no nearer a battle than the front row of a Sylvester Stallone movie. Ludicrously implausible as his achievements were, Stallone's epic posing had a considerable effect upon young males feeling increasingly emasculated both by a society which seemed able to dispense with the services of many of them, and by a shift in female attitudes which undermined traditional gender roles.

For such men, the dress of the soldier, the trappings of overt masculinity, provided a second-hand virility, a surrogate identity and a safety net for uncertainties. They began to wear items of dress which helped to reinforce their masculinity: chains and studs, peaked caps, Nazi insignia and regalia, slogan-daubed leather, leopardskin wrist-bands. All of these, along with shaved heads, can be seen as either offensive or pathetic, but they were an easy and quick 'fix' on the new masculinity – easier, certainly, than achieving a body of the fascist perfection of Arnold Schwarzenegger's.

In the 1980s such second-hand heroics were subsumed in the trend for non-status dressing which came as a reaction to that decade's designer-label craze. For men who had no interest in such status games, sportswear chic took over. The military and the sporting are of course remarkably closely linked. As romantic symbols of virility, modern sports heroes are the new militia. Like soldiers, they need fitness, courage, determination, endurance and the will to win. As sports become increasingly competitive, and financial rewards reach astronomical levels, the concepts of self-control and fair play, which are still meant to play an important role in creating the military persona, have been virtually lost in the sports arena. The ethics of the sport are now subservient to the man, and top sportsmen are treated to such a level of hero worship that the young, the immature and the inadequate inevitably wish to buy into their world by adopting both their dress and their manner. It is for this reason that designer labels became such a fetish in the eighties on the terraces and in the stadiums. Rich young footballers, along with city and media types – all of whom had ample amounts of disposable wealth – did what all the upwardly mobile do: they used their money to buy what they saw as class. And that meant labels. Where they led, fans followed. The designers who most caught the imagination were the Italians, enjoying a high point of fashion fame in both women's and men's wear. Elegantly opulent or sophisticatedly minimalist, their boutiques and shops sprang up wherever the rich were to be found, from Rodeo Drive to Sloane Square. A vast industry in fake designer wear was also born for those who felt unable to pay the prices demanded but who refused to be denied the cachet of the designer name. The leaders of the pack, rivals for the international big money spenders and the hordes who craved cheap copies, were Giorgio Armani and Gianni Versace.

Armani captured and held sales high ground for most of the eighties. He became a household name when he created the wardrobe for Richard Gere in the 1980 film *American Gigolo* – a headstart on which he capitalized with hugely expensive advertising campaigns, using the world's top photographers, and an endless series of media interviews about the man, his lifestyle and his designs. This publicity alone would probably have been enough to make clothes bearing his label so covetable that they could be priced at almost any level and still sell worldwide. Yet the reason for his success was not 'hype', but the fact that he was a designer of genius, brilliantly in tune with the mood of his time.

The basis of Armani's success was his belief in formality treated informally. He knew that the men who could afford his clothes spent all their working lives, and most of their social lives, in suits. So he gave them suits which would raise no eyebrows in the City or on Wall Street but which were traditional in neither cut nor scale. Using the lightest of materials, he deconstructed the power suit by removing excess padding, frequently omitting linings, and cutting with a generosity which enabled the wearer to feel relaxed and at ease.

Knowing, too, that one of the concerns of the stylish man was the fear of wearing a creased jacket – a serious problem with lightweight fabrics – he reintroduced linen as a menswear material and at a stroke made the creased look a source of pride rather than embarrassment.

Armani also knew that muscles were the sexual currency of young men in the eighties – young men who played squash and worked out as much to look good as for the joy of the sport. By using soft materials and shaping his jackets to fit the athletic figure, he created formal suits which, for the first time in history, clothed the torso without disguising it and responded to the body and its movements. Above all, their looseness made the wearer feel not only at ease but also sexually charged.

Where Armani led, others followed. His designs trickled down to all levels of fashion and all price ranges. Suddenly, the majority of men's suits and jackets were deconstructed. Armani exerted greater influence on menswear than any other designer of the eighties, but his designs were so minimalist that they could not be improved upon. In a decade when most clothes were over-designed, his appeared to the

ABOVE: Classic Armani, from his 1996–97 collection. Photo by Peter Lindbergh

uninitiated to be under-designed. And his minimalism was an end in itself: like a building's neoclassical façade, it was based on rules which, if altered, were necessarily debased. It could not move forward because there was nowhere for it to go without destroying itself.

Fashion is always nervous of standing still for too long. It needs to move on. Armani's day as the foremost menswear influence ended with the decade. In the nineties Gianni Versace took the lead. No two designers could be more different. Armani's restraint seemed over-refined when compared with Versace's ebullience. Where Armani worked with muted colour and minimal pattern, Versace's colour and pattern rioted across everything he did. The hot pigments of the Ballets Russes, the strong geometrics of medieval Italian flags and pennants, the oblique references to Warhol's multicoloured animal prints, the East, South America, African tribal masks, Aboriginal body patterning – Versace's creative antennae were tuned to everything. He took his motifs from all over the globe and all periods of history in order to give menswear a dazzle and colour never seen before in such total saturation.

Like Armani, Versace was fixated on the male body and much of his design approach could be read as homoerotic, even sado-masochistic. His working of leather frequently revealed a touch of genius. If an Armani suit was a collector's item, a Versace black leather blouson or pair of pants were museum pieces. Indeed, in a moment of over-excitement, the historian Sir Roy Strong

confessed that he hoped to be buried in his Versace trousers, they so fitted his ideal of perfection.

But, of course, for every man – footballer, city gent or man of culture – who could afford designer labels, there were thousands who took advantage of the new approaches by deformalizing themselves at a much cheaper level. If designer labels were the shorthand for the status of wealth, the T-shirt was the archetypal item of egalitarian clothing. The two seem miles apart, but clever marketing techniques brought them together with resounding success.

Just when the slogan T-shirt was becoming a bore for all but teenagers, it was transformed into something much more sophisticated – a walking advertisement not merely for a designer's product but also for the class and clout of the wearer. Status was conferred on a plain cotton T-shirt merely by adding a designer's name. Calvin Klein jeans and DKNY (Donna Karan New York), like Ralph Lauren's Polo logo, spell status worldwide and it seems entirely appropriate that all three are American – after all, America was the country which invented publicity and, more than one hundred years ago, set menswear on the path of informality, youth and fitness which will clearly carry it forward for the next hundred.

The progression from tailor-inspired to designer-led male fashion which began in the 1960s has now come to full fruition. Menswear is currently as designer-dominated as womenswear. But, unlike women's fashion, there is little consensus; there is a wider range of men's styles than in any other area of fashion. What is on offer is not confined to any one country or culture. Design attitudes criss-cross the globe. An American designer might well have more in common with someone working in Paris than with his U.S. colleagues. A Japanese designer might find himself working along identical lines to a designer in London. More obviously than in womenswear, male fashion springs from a wide variety of philosophies and preoccupations.

All menswear designers have one thing in common, however. They are attempting to answer the question: How should the end-of-the-millennium male clothe himself in order to reflect his masculine strength, position in society and relationship with women? Times have never been harder for men. If they do not know what part they should be playing, how can they know how to dress for it? At the end of the century, when dress has become a central preoccupation for all men and an obsession for some, many men searching for a self-image are still alarmed at the thought of being fashionable and are frightened by the idea of changing style as frequently as they imagine women do.

It is still not clear how much the majority of men need or want fashion. Informality is now a way of life and fashion is increasingly confined to a pair of chinos or jeans, worn with a sweatshirt and a pair of trainers. But, viewing the menswear collections from the top designers, it is hard to believe that this will continue. There are more

exciting alternatives in male dress than at any time in history. Though the majority of men ignore them, with every season all but the most arcane move a little closer to general, mainstream fashion. Male attitudes to dress change more slowly than those of women, so much so that it has taken more than twenty years for something as innocuous as the male earring to become accepted, and even now it is confined to casual, off-duty wear, just as brightly coloured shirts and aggressively patterned ties were not so long ago. Class attitudes, such as snobbery and the fear of vulgarity, have always played a large part in the male response to clothing and they are no less prominent today. Men still hold extremely firm views as to what is suitable male dress.

In fact, male social attitudes at the end of the twentieth century parallel female attitudes a hundred years ago. Then, for women to wear trousers was seen as eccentricity, or, worse, as an attempt to undermine the foundations of society. Few could have imagined that within a century trousers would have become not only acceptable but also fashionable. Will the next hundred years see men making a similar leap and wearing skirts as casually as they now wear trousers?

If they do, it will be a vindication of the persistence of Jean-Paul Gaultier, the most radical and uncompromising designer working in male fashion today. Totally committed to cross-gender dressing, he sends striding down his runway strapping young white men in sarongs and feather boas, and butch blacks in leopardskin and rubies. The effect is challenging, invigorating and, to judge by the reaction of the women in his audience, sexually exciting. He destroys the orthodoxy of gender stereotype with flair and unwavering conviction, despite the fact that 90 percent of his ideas for male dress die on the catwalk.

It would be easy to dismiss the eclectic and technically brilliant Gaultier as an eccentric whose fashion has no relevance to the realities of male dress. But to do so would be wrong. If any menswear designer can be said to be leading us forward by changing male attitudes to self, it must be Jean-Paul Gaultier. In as little as fifty years time he may well be seen as the only designer of vision at the end of the twentieth century.

Not that he stands entirely alone. The designer John Bartlett is often claimed as the Gaultier of U.S. menswear. Like Gaultier, Bartlett believes in the power of nudity and the allure of the male body. A Harvard graduate and a product of the Fashion Institute of Technology, he brings to his work the wide cultural references and historic awareness found also in Gaultier's menswear.

Both Gaultier and Bartlett design clothes with attitude for men with attitude. But the majority of men prefer clothes which do not pose questions. They want to dress unexceptionally, taking comfort in an appearance that makes them part of a group. To answer their needs, modern fashion has combined the best of the old-guard Savile Row formality with the relaxed assurance of the Armani approach to create clothes which have been described as perfect for making money in. The top name in this lucrative field is probably Hugo Boss, a German firm with an international profile. Founded in 1923 to make working clothes and uniforms, Boss has a modern style which combines power dressing with a touch of gangster flash. The entrepreneurial quality of Boss clothes appeals on both sides of the Atlantic. Entirely appropriately, it was Boss which provided the clothes for the male actors in the 1980s television programmes *L.A. Law* and *Miami Vice*.

More traditional firms producing the same type of affluent dress for the relatively successful middle-aged man are English menswear companies such as Aquascutum, Simpson's and Burberry, and the Italian family concern of Ermenegildo Zegna, founded in 1910, which sells around 300,000 suits a year at prices only slightly below those of Armani or Versace. Other companies in this high-class bracket, providing formal suits, traditionally tailored but with a modern sensibility, using classic materials such as tweed, worsted and flannel, include Nino Cerruti, described by *L'Uomo Vogue* in 1990 as creating clothes with an 'elegant simplicity that doesn't smack too much of fashion'; Brioni, whose hand-sewn suits are as carefully crafted as were those they custom-made in the fifties for actors like Clark Gable and Kirk Douglas; and Corneliani, Alan Flusser and Adolfo Dominguez.

Younger men want something more radical. They turn to designers like Dolce & Gabbana, seen by many as the most original design team working in Italy today. Their women's clothes are provocatively sexy; their menswear explores the range of male power and assurance. Although international and sophisticated, their menswear contains an endearingly rough-hewn element of country provincialism, accentuated by the hand-crafted quality of the workmanship and detailing. These are subtle clothes, far removed from the high gloss of much Italian male fashion.

Dolce & Gabbana are the leaders of a broad-based approach to male dressing whose exponents are found across the world. The American designer Joseph Abboud, who once worked with Ralph Lauren, takes their organic country feel and refines it to break through the town-country barrier with an emphasis on ethnic colours and texture. His clothes, often layered, have a hand-crafted quality which gives them a relaxed assurance which appeals to men with the same characteristics. Andrew Fezza, another American and a cult figure for many, amalgamates in his work respect for the integrity of fabric and the laid-back fluidity of cut characteristic of Armani's directional work in the eighties. A major talent, Fezza has a design approach which is as advanced as Gaultier's, though less shocking and spectacular – it

probably answers the needs of sophisticated men better than anything else being produced in the nineties.

There is strong competition to these American designers, not least from Britain and Europe. One of the unexpected fashion developments of the late eighties was the emergence of Belgium as a design force. Belgian design seemed to spring fully-formed onto the fashion scene with few, if any, preliminaries. Dirk Bikkembergs, Ann Demeulemeester and Martin Margiela raised – and answered – challenging questions about male dress with a confidence and disregard for tradition reminiscent of the new-wave Japanese designers of the early eighties.

After the first searing shock of a new approach, the Belgian designers have gone forward to become a major influence in menswear. Bikkembergs, who has said, 'I design collections which give one whole, strong look,' denies that his fashion approach is retro, claiming that he hates the idea of looking back. But his clothes – macho, tough and aggressive – do in fact articulate traditional notions of peasant masculinity. They have been copied internationally by mass-market manufacturers aiming at the young male market.

Bikkembergs' toughness has been hugely influential but it is perhaps Ann Demeulemeester who has most successfully captured the spirit of the nineties in her approach to menswear. She has adapted the early eighties Japanese avant-garde approach to fit and cut in order to create

ABOVE: Design for Dolce & Gabbana, 1993–94

her own austerity. Martin Margiela has taken deconstruction to its limits in his sliced, cut and filleted approach. He was labelled a maverick with his first collection in 1989, and his clothes were dubbed 'Le mode destroy'. But such a negative tag misses the point of his radicalism. Like Gaultier, with whom he trained, Margiela questions and codifies in order to find an authentic approach to modern dress, free of all links with historicism. He has created jackets from plastic bin liners and sweaters from old army socks but his clothes are much more than mere flea-market chic. With their dangling threads, exposed linings and frayed surfaces, they emphasize the craftsmanship of fashion creativity while exposing the pretensions and fallibilities of more mainstream fashion. Like Franco Moschino, Margiela shows his contempt for fashion orthodoxy in every item he designs.

Moschino's design slogan, 'Stop the Fashion System', suffered the irony of itself becoming fashionable, which would have pleased Italy's irreverent *enfant terrible*, who died in 1994. Irony was his stock-in-trade. Although he was not interested in the question of gender, Moschino was a master of parody and shared Gaultier's conviction that witty clothes can make memorable and important points. His menswear was exuberantly camp, full of verbal and visual puns. Straitjacket shirts were emblazoned 'For fashion victims only'; he produced pastiches of the work of other designers, commenting, for example, on the banality of much commercial

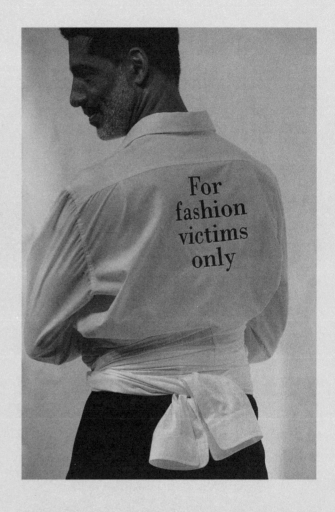

fashion of the Calvin Klein type by producing his own line of underpants, worn on top of trousers and bearing the waistband slogan 'To Be Shown in Public'. His 'the joker is wild' approach brought him enormous publicity: Moschino jeans became one of Europe's biggest sellers in the late 1980s. What made his clothes so joyful was his bold approach to colour and pattern, his American-style fifties tailoring and, above all, his love of Surrealism, expressed in jackets covered in Magritte clouds, in Mickey Mouse waistcoats and in the use of *faux* animal skin.

ABOVE: Moschino's straitjacket shirt, 1994

Moschino's playful quality was echoed on a much more commercial level by Alan Cleaver and Keith Varty of Byblos. Their bold approach to solid colour appealed to a young market, as did their jokey reworking of old stereotypes of super-masculinity from cowboys to the Marrakesh of Rudolph Valentino. Though no longer with Byblos – their place was taken by Richard Tyler in 1996 – they continue to design.

The avant garde is not the province of Paris and Italy alone. In fact, it still finds its fullest flowering in London. Almost as if in deliberate contrast to the traditional approach for which London male fashion has long been known, young menswear designers take a consistently iconoclastic and irreverent stance.

Clothes are never simple. By articulating the attitudes of society they become part of the politics of that society. Nowhere is this seen more clearly than in Britain, still the most class-conscious nation in the world. As if in opposition to this, most of the vibrancy of young British fashion, and, for that matter, of 'Brit-pop' music, springs from defiance of class barriers. The appeal of clothes by Wayne Hemingway of Red or Dead is like the music of Oasis – resolutely working class and overtly hostile to upper-class mores, including attitudes to taste. The Red or Dead approach is about a new kind of power dressing – one which harnesses the raw energy and anger of 'hard times' street fashion and turns it into what has been called recession chic. Red or Dead has done this with humour and individuality and

nowhere more successfully than in Hemingway's early variations on Doc Marten footwear. Brilliantly coloured, often in Dayglo shades or silver, in mock-patent or perspex, sometimes printed with Op Art patterns or covered with animal skin prints, they are a statement of defiant faith in the power of bad taste.

Perhaps even more influential in London – certainly during the middle years of the 1980s – was the design team of Richmond and Cornejo. Working within a darker and more dangerous sensibility than that of Hemingway, they took the dress of S&M out of the specialist clubs and made it a fashion look for the streets under their label 3D, which stood for Destroy, Disorientate and Disorder. Their clothes were a deliberately provocative questioning of sexual stereotypes. Tightly cut rubber and leather emphasized male as well as female curves and was given an added sexual frisson by the use of zippers, safety pins and studs as fastenings.

The camp quality of Richmond/Cornejo links with that of another English designer, Stephen Linard, whose first show at St Martin's School of Art in 1981 caused a sensation. Called 'Reluctant Emigrés', it was a statement about fashion and gender. Linard used as models tough East Enders with no graces or catwalk skills. Unwashed, stubbled, tattooed and sideburned, they brought a raw, crude masculinity to his diaphanous organza shirts, swirling great coats with astrakhan collars and provocatively patched trousers. The juxtapositions were a *coup de théâtre*, spawning the New Romantics club dress worn most successfully by the musician Boy George, with whom Linard had shared a squat, and the club personality Leigh Bowery.

If this was theatricality pushed dangerously close to fancy dress, the early 1980s London fashion scene, with its strong anti-Establishment bias, attracted designers who knew how to harness the new approaches and feelings in a way that would reach the Establishment without alarming it. Scott Crolla and Paul Smith were the men who tamed radical anti-fashion sufficiently for it to sell. Crolla, who was originally part of a team with Georgina Godley, created fabric-based fashion in which line and detail was secondary to colour and pattern. Taking the New Romanticism of the clubs, Crolla softened it into a wearable form of dandyism suitable for drawing rooms. Rich brocades, velvet and embroidery, Indian silks and cotton shirts printed with flowers – the effect was part-eighteenth-century, part-thirties-Colonialist and remarkably similar in spirit to the dress of the swinging sixties pop world.

Paul Smith's approach was much more commercially strong. He created a look which combined traditional menswear with a modern viewpoint to make himself one of the London menswear designers whose clothes were – and are – trusted by those traditionally afraid of the concept of male fashion. Never risible, outrageous or effeminate, Smith's clothes nevertheless had humour and just the right

degree of cheeky colour combinations, jokey pattern mixes and cartoony design motifs. Though he has often been compared to Ralph Lauren, all they have in common is a shrewdly entrepreneurial skill in assessing a mood, detoxifying it and marketing it in a way that is irresistible to status seekers. Such skills have made Smith a household name and given him cult status in Japan.

Men in the West do not find it as easy to understand Japanese fashion. The reason for this is a fundamental one: Japanese design is timeless and ageless whereas Western fashion is predicated on the need for rapid change. It follows that Western fashion is dominated by commercial interests in a way that Japanese fashion is not. Japanese fashion allows itself a time span in which clothes that might possibly be considered works of art can be created.

And if there is a Japanese designer who is creating them, it is the visionary Issey Miyake, who turns the clothed body into a piece of living sculpture. As with all sculpture, shape is important and colour secondary; pattern is primary, texture essential. Miyake's clothes have an organic, timeless quality which makes them independent of their surroundings. Whether they are 'modern' or 'new' – crucial questions in Western fashion – is irrelevant. They could have been worn five hundred years ago and they would still look right today. They could be worn five hundred years from now and they would not look old-fashioned.

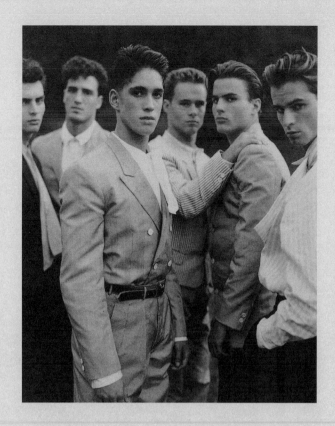

Esoteric, exotic, 'difficult' as Miyake is considered to be by those who have not worn his clothes, those who *have* worn them (young and old) find them an exhilarating and liberating experience. He has his followers and his disciples. Chief among the latter are Rei Kawakubo of Comme des Garçons and Yohji Yamamoto, both of whom have adopted the Miyake philosophy to make their own powerful menswear statements. The minimalist Kawakubo works largely in monochrome. Her cutting, seaming and stitching justify her cryptic comment on her technique: 'I give the fabric history.'

In Kawakubo's severely limited palette for menswear, black predominates. Yamamoto is altogether more flamboyant. He chooses his motifs from Japan – the Kabuki theatre; and from the West – post-Punk deconstruction – to create a colourful world of menswear which can often disguise the fact that his sensibilities are anchored in neither the East nor the West, though his clothes do have a youthful lack of

sophistication which links him more convincingly with the West.

America is the most powerful consumer nation not only in the West, but also in the world. Its fashion philosophy is based on casual, relaxed clothes which, to the outsider, appear to be a negation of status dress. Many of the firms supplying these clothes do not even employ a designer. Most are long-established as manufacturers of utilitarian workwear and sportswear. These include athletic firms such as British Knights, Nautico, Cross Colours and, most popular of all, Champion, founded by two sporting brothers in 1919 and now one of the largest suppliers of sportswear in the world. A Champion sweatshirt is a cult item, worn by college students and kids on the block as well as by amateur and professional athletes. The 1992 U.S. Olympic basketball team chose Champion as its official supplier of games kit.

It is because a Champion garment trails such illustrious associations that, unlike designer wear, its practicality is enhanced with age. Nobody ever throws away a Champion sweatshirt. Everybody knows that it only really comes into its own after at least five years of active wear, by which time, frayed and faded but perfectly comfortable, it has become part of a man's personal life and tradition. Such clothing, which commands loyalty from men who have no interest in fashion, is not unique to the United States. British firms like Burberry, Simpson's – who produce the Daks range – and Aquascutum were traditionally geared to the needs of the country sportsman who wanted tough clothing, proof against terrain, temperature and climate; clothing which would survive all and never wear out. It was essentially dress for gentlemen and their senior servants, such as ghillies and gamekeepers. In North America, hunting, shooting and fishing were not exclusive pleasures of the rich; safeguarded by law, they were every citizen's right. American sportswear manufacturers reflect that egalitarianism. L.L. Bean, founded in Maine in 1912, produced practical hunting wear for ordinary men with no thought of creating anything stylish, let alone fashionable. Leon Leonwood Bean was an inventor as well as a sportsman and he used his skills to improve on traditional items of dress. He attracted and kept a loyal following by his practical approach, which included opening for business three hundred and sixty-five days a year. Much of his trade was through mail order and his catalogues became a byword for quirkiness. L.L. Bean has literally clothed the American Dream of the country life for almost a century.

The philosophy of sportswear has been the basis for many other American companies, long-established firms like L.C. Penny, or recent concerns like The Gap and Banana Republic. The Gap has triumphantly proved the importance of focus in this market. Founded in 1969, the original Gap shop in San Francisco sold Levi jeans and pop records so successfully that it went on to market its own brand-name clothes.

The Gap's triumph is as much one of retailing and advertising as it is of designing. As the personification of the quintessential American spirit, it appeals to both sexes and all ages, regardless of ethnic or geographical differences.

It is possible that firms specializing in sports and casual wear may lead the field in male dress by the end of the millennium. Of all the varieties of clothing on offer to men today, garments which are largely anonymous, practical and less vulnerable to stylistic change seem to have the greatest appeal. This should not surprise us, given men's conformist nature and their need to bond with other men through dress. At the end of the century even the man of fashion finds the extremes of high fashion contrived, unattractive and unwearable. The majority of men prefer casual, active sportswear. Increasingly, they draw their status not from designer labels, but from their work, their physique and their social position.

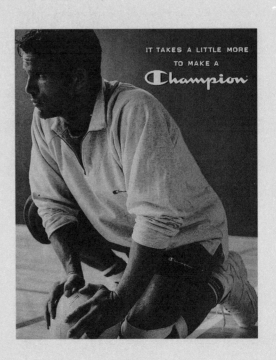

RIGHT: Advertisement for Champion sportswear, 1996

ACKNOWLEDGMENTS

The publishers would like to thank the following for their help in the preparation of this book, and in particular the designers and companies who generously made available original sketches and photographs from their archives.

ALAN ABOUD and MAXINE LAW of Aboud·Sodano, GIORGIO ARMANI, DIRK BIKKEMBERGS, HUGO BOSS, BRIONI, BURBERRY, PAUL CARANICAS, PIERRE CARDIN, CERRUTI, CHAMPION, COMME DES GARÇONS, DOLCE & GABBANA, JEAN-PAUL GAULTIER, TOM GILBEY, MADAME M.T. HIRSCHKOFF, ELIZABETH KERR of Camera Press, CALVIN KLEIN, RALPH LAUREN, ANGELO LITRICO, GAI PEARL MARSHALL of Pearl Design Associates, MISSONI, JOHN RICHMOND, YVES SAINT LAURENT, PAUL SMITH, RICHARD TYLER, VALENTINO and GIANNI VERSACE.

Special thanks are due to ROBERT GIEVE, of Gieves and Hawkes, for providing information about both Savile Row and the finer points of men's tailoring. We are also grateful to MOSS BROS for giving us permission to use some drawings from their 1960s booklet *Beau Brummell Was Right*, by James Laver, and to JOHN PEACOCK for kindly lending us his copy of that publication.

Finally, we would like to thank NIALL MCINERNEY for making his photographic archives available to us and for patiently answering our many questions.

PHOTOGRAPHIC ACKNOWLEDGMENTS

AKG, London 12 *top right*
Alinari, Florence 89
Allsport UK Ltd 123 *bottom*
Arizona Historical Society, Tucson, Arizona 126
Courtesy of Giorgio Armani 182, 194
Nick Baratha/Sportswear International 156 *bottom*
Barnaby's Picture Library, London 12 *bottom right*, 151
Collection Biagiotti–Cigna, Guidonia 156
Biblioteca Ambrosiana, Milan 28
Bibliothèque des Arts Décoratifs, Paris 48
Bibliothèque Nationale, Paris 22 *bottom*, 47
Bibliothèque Royale, Brussels 27, 29, 30
Courtesy of Dirk Bikkembergs 164, 165
Courtesy of Hugo Boss 160 *bottom*
Bowes Museum, Barnard Castle 18 *left*
Bridgeman Art Library 20, 21, 161 *top*
Courtesy of Brioni, Rome 135
British Film Institute 132 *top*, 166 *bottom*
British Museum, London 52, 55 *both*, 58 *all*, 59 *all*, 72, 74
Bulloz, Paris 57
Burghley House, National Trust 181 *centre*
Camera Press 167 *top*, 180 *centre left*
Camera Press/John Hedgecoe 22, Karsh of Ottawa 23 *left*
Carlton Publications 2 *right*
Courtesy of Paul Caranicas. All Rights Reserved 170, 191
Courtesy of Pierre Cardin, Paris 144 *both*
Courtesy of Cerruti 1881, Menswear 164
Courtesy of Champion, USA 203
J.L. Charmet, Paris 14 *top*, 48
J.L. Charmet, Paris © ADAGP, Paris and DACS, London 1997 23 *top*
Courtesy of Comme des Garçons 202
Dinodia Picture Agency, Bombay 177
Courtesy of Dolce & Gabbana 159, 198
Mary Evans Picture Library 85, 100, 101, 130 *top*, 135 *bottom right*
Mary Evans Picture Library © ADAGP, Paris and DACS, London 1997 181 *top*
Galleria Nazionale, Rome 24
Courtesy of Jean-Paul Gaultier 128 *top* and *left*

Gemäldegalerie, Dresden 12
Germanisches Nationalmuseum, Nuremberg 26
Courtesy of Gieves and Hawkes, London 94, 95 *inset*
Courtesy of Tom Gilbey 60
Stevie Hughes/*Arena* 168
Hulton Getty Picture Collection 66, 67 *both*, 71 *inset*, 91, 130 *right*, 131, 141
Hutchison Picture Library 11, 99 *bottom right*
André Kertész Estate, New York 92 *top*
Courtesy of Calvin Klein 175
Kunsthistorisches Museum, Vienna 17
Courtesy of Ralph Lauren 97, 165 *top*
Library of Congress, Washington DC 81, 83 *bottom*, 97 *bottom*, 109, 113
Courtesy of Angelo Litrico 139
Niall McInerney 14, 16, 61 *centre, left to right*, 70, 90, 98 *top*, 102 *top*, 103, 123 *top*, 124 *bottom left*, 125, 153, 154 *bottom*, 155 *top*, 157 *top*, 158, 163, 165 *bottom*, 166 *top*, 180 *bottom right*, 182, 183, 185 *centre* and *bottom right*, 188 *bottom right*, 189, 192
Magnum/Briggs 132 *centre left*/Martine Franck 178
Mas, Barcelona 12, 181 *bottom*
Merseyside County Art Galleries 34, 156–7
© Lee Miller Archive, Chiddingly, East Sussex 98 *right*
Courtesy of Missoni, Milan 133 *top* and *bottom*
Chris Moore 62, 70 *top*, 102 *bottom*, 124 *top*, 184 *bottom right*, 185 *top right*, 188 *left* and *top right*, 190 *top left*
Courtesy of Moss Bros Ltd 54, 87
Courtesy of Moschino 61, 199
Ugo Mulas, Electa 178
Musée d'Art Moderne, Paris 23
Musée des Beaux Arts, Liège 57
National Gallery, London 10, 13, 37, 63, 66
National Maritime Museum, Greenwich 129 *top*
National Portrait Gallery, London 22, 68, 71 *top*, 132 *bottom, both*, 133
National Trust of Scotland 99 *centre*
Nationalgalerie, Berlin 9
New York State Historical Association 104

Courtesy of Henry Poole & Co, London 94
Popperfoto 161 *bottom right*, 162
Prado Museum, Madrid 12, 181
Private Collection 44
H.M. The Queen 19, 35
© Man Ray Trust/ADAGP, Paris and DACS, London 1997 166 *top centre*
Redferns 69, 121, 178 *bottom right*
Réunion des Musées Nationaux, Paris 78
Courtesy of John Richmond 186
Derek Ridgers/*The Face* 179
Roger-Viollet, Paris 100 *left*, 136
Ronald Grant Archive 91 *top* and *right*, 119, 127, 129, 134–5, 158–9, 160–1, 167, 190
F.D. Roosevelt Library, Washington DC 96
Paolo Roversi/Studio Luce 184 *top* and *left*
Royal Photographic Society 71
Courtesy of Yves Saint Laurent 15
August Sander Archiv, SK Stiftung Kultur, Cologne © DACS 1997 93
Scala, Florence 16 *bottom*, 34, 161
Editore Sellerio, Palermo from 'L'età dei Florio', 1985 92, 122
Gotthard Shah 128 *bottom right*
Courtesy of Paul Smith Ltd, illustration Aboud•Sodano 99 *top right*
Tom of Finland/Benedikt Taschen Verlag 10
Topham Picturepoint 116, 146
Courtesy of Richard Tyler 19
Nunes Vais/ICCD, Rome 22 *top left*
Courtesy of Valentino 190 *bottom right*
Courtesy of Gianni Versace 166 *top right*
Musées de Versailles 20, 21
Victoria and Albert Museum, London 180 *top*
Andy Warhol Foundation, New York © ARS, New York and DACS, London 1997 127 *bottom*
Writers and Readers Publ. Inc. New York, from R.S. Roberts, 'A True Likeness', 1994, 187

Every effort has been made to trace the copyright owners of photographs included in this book. Any inadvertent omission should be brought to the attention of the publishers.

INDEX